THE MAZEPPA LEGEND
IN EUROPEAN ROMANTICISM

HORACE VERNET, *Mazeppa Aux Loups* The Tokyo 1832
PHOTOGRAPH TAKEN FROM AN ENGRAVING

HUBERT F. BABINSKI

The *MAZEPPA LEGEND In EUROPEAN ROMANTICISM*

Columbia University Press / New York & London

1974

THE ANDREW W. MELLON FOUNDATION,
THROUGH A SPECIAL GRANT, HAS ASSISTED
THE PRESS IN PUBLISHING THIS VOLUME.

Library of Congress Cataloging in Publication Data
Babinski, Hubert F. 1936–
The Mazeppa legend in European romanticism.
Bibliography: p.
1. Mazepa, Ivan Stepanovyeh, Hetman of the Cossacks,
1644–1709, in fiction, drama, poetry, etc.
2. Mazepa, Ivan Stepanovyeh, Hetman of the Cossacks,
1644–1709—Portraits, caricatures, etc.
3. Mazepa, Ivan Stepanovyeh, Hetman of the Cossacks, 1644–1709—
Songs and music—History and criticism.
4. Romanticism in art. I. Title.
NX652.M3B32   809'.933'51   74–6152
ISBN 0–231–03825–9

To my Mother and Father

PREFACE

I SHOULD LIKE to acknowledge the help and advice I received from my friends and colleagues at the Institute of Literary Research in Warsaw and to the Institute itself for allowing me to use its libraries for all these years. The Columbia University Libraries were an aid and comfort to me because they always managed to get the material I needed so rapidly. I also want to offer my thanks to the librarians at the Slavic Collection of the New York Public Library and to the staff of the Ukrainian Library in New York City.

I am especially grateful to Professors Harold B. Segel and Carl Woodring for their help, advice, and encouragement. To them as my teachers, colleagues, and friends, I owe a great deal more than this book.

Professors Frederick Keener and William McBrien were kind enough and patient enough to read my manuscript and to give me many suggestions that substantially changed the final form of this book. I thank them for their honest criticism and good natures.

Although there were many who contributed materially and spiritually to this book, I should like to thank especially Professor Beatrice Nosco for the help she gave me with the Swedish translations and Columbia University for the financial aid it gave me to have the final draft typed.

CONTENTS

THE MAZEPPA LEGEND
IN EUROPEAN ROMANTICISM

INTRODUCTION

IVAN MAZEPPA was a prominent figure in European Romantic poetry, painting, and music, yet he has received scant attention in nineteenth-century studies. His name may bring to mind Byron's Oriental Tale *Mazeppa*, or Hugo's lyric in *Les Orientales*, or more likely conjure images of Adah Menken, lashed to a white stallion, treading the boards of a provincial American theater in the late nineteenth century. Few, however, know that Mazeppa was actually a seventeenth-century Cossack leader and the subject of works by Géricault, Delacroix, Liszt, Ryleev, Pushkin, and the Polish Romantic poet Juliusz Słowacki, among others less familiar. Nor do they know that he is the major character of epic and narrative poems, lyrics, ballads, paintings, equestrian dramas, ballets, tragedies, and even puppet shows of the Romantic era.

The significance of Mazeppa in European Romanticism has not been recognized before because, when considered only in a national context— for example in English or in Slavic Romanticism—the theme seems like one tile in a large mosaic. However, when looked at in the context of Europe, and from a comparatist's point of view, it forms a rich, extensive, varied pattern of its own; it is a theme of major dimensions. Mazeppa is especially interesting thematically because his use by Romantic artists illustrates so clearly the transformation of a historical figure with legendary overtones into a mythic-messianic hero. As poets and painters add to and refine the mythmaking process, one can almost chart their attempts to create verbal and visual symbols from Mazeppa and his life. One can follow an artist's reworking of his predecessors' treatments of the theme, and in nearly every case that artist's successful transcendence of his influences. Ivan Mazeppa, then, was not merely a static subject for the European Romantics; he acted as an imaginative catalyst, and the works in which he appears are excellent for comprehending the dynamics of a particular Romantic artist's mind.

Mazeppa was born in Polish-Ukrainian territory in 1632 or 1644, depending upon whose evidence one accepts, and died in 1709 in Bender, Moldavia, a few months after he and Charles XII of Sweden were defeated at the Battle of Poltava by Peter I. As a youth he spent five or six years as a page in the Court of the Polish King Jan Kazimierz, and some dubious historical accounts suggest that Mazeppa probably had to leave Poland as a young man because he became entangled in a love intrigue with the wife of a Polish nobleman. The one event of his life that achieved wide notoriety in the eighteenth and nineteenth centuries was allegedly the result of this amorous involvement. The Polish nobleman purportedly banished Mazeppa by having him strapped naked to a wild horse and sent off to the steppes to die. The story goes that he was saved by peasants and eventually rose to be Hetman of the Ukraine (the title refers to an East European ruler whose power and status lay somewhere between a king's and a chief's). That legend was central to Romantic works about Mazeppa, but there is no solid historical evidence to support such a dramatic banishment.

About ten years after he left the Polish Court, however, he did suddenly appear in the Cossack army of a Ukrainian general where he did work his way through the ranks to become Hetman. While a senior officer he became a confidant of Peter I, who at the time was using Cossack armies against Charles XII, who was then sweeping across Europe in hopes of subjugating Russia. For motives that remain uncertain, Mazeppa as Hetman decided to conspire with Charles XII against his friend Peter I; and in July 1709 the Czar conquered the combined armies of the Cossacks and Swedes at the Battle of Poltava. The defeated rulers fled to Moldavia, where Mazeppa died shortly thereafter, and where Charles XII intrigued for years to return to Sweden. Mazeppa's odd life, with its twists of character and fate, became a source of folk literature immediately after his death.

He has been the subject of art works from the seventeenth century to the present, but the first half of the nineteenth century was the heyday of his popularity. Although Mazeppa lived and died in Eastern Europe, his name and exploits first reached an international audience in 1731, when Voltaire published *Histoire de Charles XII*, in which Mazeppa's wild ride into exile is briefly described. Voltaire's analysis of Charles XII's political rise and fall, plus the controversy over the factual sources of the book, caused it to be a minor literary sensation in the courts and salons of Europe. Its readers learned substantially little about Hetman Mazeppa from Roxolania, then the Latin name for the Ukrainian territory, but the book did stimulate the curiosity of Europeans about Mazeppa and Eastern Europe. Voltaire's short account of Mazeppa's life was more hearsay than fact, and in the 1760s André Dorville, a minor though prolific French novelist, enriched the legend by further fictionalizing the few facts in his *Mémoires d'Azéma*. Dorville's Mazeppa is a hero *manqué* with the sensibility of a man of feeling who was so appealing to late-eighteenth-century readers. In 1819 Lord Byron refashioned Dorville's hero in *Mazeppa*, in which the legend of Mazeppa's wild ride, his meteoric rise to fame and power, and his defeat at Poltava come together in a long poem that became the source for most Romantic treatments of the Mazeppa theme in Europe. Victor Hugo and the painters in his circle added the finishing touches to what I designate the Western legend of Mazeppa by turning him into a symbol of the Romantic artist.

Another legend of Mazeppa began in the Ukrainian lands of Eastern Europe during his Hetmanate and was based more factually on the events of his life. The Ukrainians, Poles, and Russians were more fascinated by his dealings with Peter I than with his alleged wild ride, and differed in their interpretations of his politics: one camp considered him an open enemy of Russia and the Czar—a traitor; a second made him into a Ukrainian hero who had done his utmost to form the peoples of the Don and Dnieper rivers region, later called the Ukraine, into an independent political unity. The latter group felt that he had betrayed Peter I for the cause of national liberty. Peter I was, in fact, so incensed by Mazeppa's turnabout that he had the Hetman's name pronounced anathema throughout Russia; his orders were faithfully carried out from 1709 to 1917. Mazeppa's admirers, on the other hand, formed a revolutionary group called the Mazeppists and began a long underground struggle for Ukrainian independence in Eastern Europe. Two hundred years after the Battle of Poltava Mazeppist still meant either traitor or freedom fighter, depending upon one's political leanings.

Eastern European Romantics based their interpretations of Mazeppa on historical materials gathered during the later years of his life and during the eighteenth and nineteenth centuries, as well as from works of art that had already manipulated—for personal or political reasons—the facts as they became available. Furthermore, whatever survives from the late seventeenth century and early eighteenth century is due by and large to the oversight of Peter I's marauders who burned and effaced anything connected with Mazeppa or bearing his name, so that what does remain gives at best a fragmented image of the man. As for many of the historical materials themselves, they are either biased against him because most histories were written under the aegis of the Czar, who insisted upon Mazeppa's treachery, or they were inspired by Ukrainian nationalists, who deliberately slanted the facts in Mazeppa's favor. Even today Mazeppa is an enigmatic figure in Eastern European history, as his political motivation and personal integrity remain obscure in the light of recent historical evidence. The Eastern European Romantic artist, faced with such conflicting evidence, was ultimately forced to decide to treat Mazeppa heroically or treacherously on the basis of his own political allegiance and sometimes because of political expediency.

One may get the impression that the Western and Eastern legends remained distinct during the Romantic era; actually there was considerable influence from West to East. The Eastern legend had no bearing upon the West because Ukrainian, Polish, and Russian literary works were not translated into Western languages during the first half of the nineteenth century, and few Westerners, exclusive of the Eastern exiles, could read those languages. Western Romantic works, on the other hand, were translated and were very popular among the intelligentsia, who often spoke and even wrote French, English, and Italian well. The uses of Mazeppa in Eastern European Romanticism demonstrate in what ways Western Romantic art influenced or was assimilated by the Eastern artists and to what extent their needs and imaginative preoccupations were alike and to what extent they differed from their Western contemporaries. The handling of the Mazeppa theme in both East and West provides a good indication of the quality and character of what has been called the Romantic imagination. I am not suggesting that such a large concept can ever be defined, but this study of Mazeppa is intended to dispel some of the mist that hovers around that term. Mazeppa proves to be an especially useful subject for such considerations, and with that in mind, I have concluded this book with some "afterthoughts" on the European Romantic imagination.

1.

MAZEPPA IN THE WEST BEFORE BYRON

THE WESTERN EUROPEAN legend of Mazeppa had different origins and took a different shape from the one that began to grow in Eastern Europe in the Hetman's lifetime. In a profound sense, the Western mind would not be so interested in Mazeppa as the Eastern, for he was born into a different culture, lived and died in the East, and was neither an ally nor an enemy of any great Western country, except of course for his alliance with Charles XII; but that pact was made far from Paris and London, in some vague country—Ruthenia or Roxolania. Westerners were so unclear about that part of the world and its inhabitants that some thought Mazeppa was a Tartar. Although some of the facts were a little confused, Mazeppa's name and exploits were known in the West in the late seventeenth and early eighteenth centuries when notices about him appeared in German, French, English, and American periodicals.[1]

The Germans, for instance, gave space to Mazeppa's politics and military tactics in his struggles with Cossack and Ukrainian insurgents, and in 1704, *Europäische Fama*, the historical-political journal in Leipzig, published a short biography of him.[2] Even earlier, in 1687–89, Foy de la Neuville, a minor French diplomat sent by his government to Muscovy

[1] Theodore Mackiw, "Mazeppa in the Light of Contemporary English and American Sources," *The Ukrainian Quarterly* 15, no. 4, pp. 346–62; "Mazeppa (1632–1709) in Contemporary German Sources," *Zapysky Naukovogo Tovarystva Imen Schevchenka* (New York, 1959), paper no. 9; "Mazeppa in the Light of Contemporary German Sources," *ZNTS* (Munich, 1963): 144. (*Zapysky Naukovogo Tovarystva Imen Shevchenka* will be abbreviated *ZNTS*.) For French references see *Gazette de France:* December 6, 1687; December 20, 1687; February 14, 1688; February 28, 1688; June 19, 1688; November 5, 1689; November 9, 1689; November 13, 1692; November 23, 1702; April 15, 1702; February 9, 1708.

[2] Dmytro Doroshenko, *Bie Ukraine und das Reich, neun jahrhunderte deutsch-ukrainische beziehungen in Spiegel der deutschen Wissenschaft und Literatur* (Leipzig, 1941), pp. 36f.

to head a commission, published a very short account of Mazeppa in a book of observations about his experiences. In a few sentences he relates that Mazeppa was elected Hetman after his predecessor was exiled to Siberia, that Mazeppa was not handsome but intelligent, and that he had been a page in Jean Casimir's Court in Poland, a country for which Mazeppa had a special affection.[3] This brief description was published at just about the time Mazeppa became Hetman, and ten years later the book was published in London.

This early information about Mazeppa is actually a digression in a much larger story—the generally increasing interest of Westerners in Eastern Europe and the Ukraine in particular, as indicated by the many histories, travel books with first-hand accounts, personal journals, memoirs, and the like that began to appear in the late seventeenth and eighteenth centuries. The first published knowledge of the Ukraine in England in the seventeenth century was Richard Knolle's *The Generall Historie of the Turks*, which went through five editions between 1603 and 1638, and underwent many revisions and editions subsequently.[4] Byron would call that book one of the most enjoyable and important in his life.[5] Between 1698 and 1812, twenty-six travel accounts of the Ukraine were published in England alone.[6] There is no need to recount the amount of such material available in Western Europe in those two centuries as the Ukrainian historians Elie Borschak and Dmytro Doroshenko have listed and described almost every written work that has any connection with their nation.[7] The amount of material is astonishing and fascinating from an historical and ethnographic point of view: it includes detailed descriptions of the people, houses, clothing, and contemporary politics. Some

---

[3] Foy de la Neuville, *Relations curieuses, et nouvelle de Moscovie. Contenant, l'état présent de cet empire. Les expéditions des Moscovites en Crimée, en 1689. Les causes des derniers révolutions. Leurs moeurs, & leur religion. Le récit d'un voyage de Spatarus, par terre à la Chine* (Paris, 1698), pp. 80–81. Jean Casimir is the French equivalent of the Polish name Jan Kazimierz.

[4] Elie Borschak, "Early Relations Between England and Ukraine," *Slovanic and East European Review* 10 (June 1931): 138.

[5] Leslie Marchand, *Byron: A Biography*, 3 vols. (New York: Knopf, 1957) 1:30.

[6] See Peter Putnam, ed., *Seven Britons in Imperial Russia 1698–1812* (Princeton: Princeton University Press, 1952), Bibliography.

[7] Elie Borschak, "L'Ukraine dans la littérature de l'Europe Occidentale," *Le Monde Slave*. See Bibliography for full reference. Dmytro Doroshenko, *A Survey of Ukrainian Historiography* (The Ukrainian Academy of Arts and Sciences in the U.S., Inc.), vols. 5–6 (1957): 1–435.

contain references to Mazeppa, but they are largely minor biographical and political details that present him as just another Hetman trying to lead a disorganized and uncultivated people.

At the beginning of the eighteenth century, Western Europe's interest in the Great Northern War and its chief combatants, Peter I and Charles XII, brought the Ukraine into greater prominence. By that time the subject was already being used in fiction and poetry as well as in historical writing. In 1715 *The History of the Wars, of his Present Majesty Charles XII. King of Sweden; From his First Landing in Denmark, to his Return from Turkey to Pomerania. by a Scots Gentleman in the Swedish Service* was published in London.[8] Defoe's accounts are fictional but include a large amount of factual and historical information. They introduce Charles XII to Western readers, and point up his heroic qualities. If these books extol Charles XII, Aaron Hill's *The Northern Star*, published in 1718, rhapsodizes about Peter I, the Northern Star of the title. By and large, the West at this time admired Peter I not only for his military prowess but for his program of "Westernization" of all the Russias instituted after he had traveled and lived in the West. Charles XII was a lesser known figure who had made dramatic victories across Europe, but of course he ultimately lost to the Czar and lived in exile for years before he made his surreptitious return to Sweden. By the time Dr. Johnson wrote *The Vanity of Human Wishes* (1749), Charles XII had lost most of his prestige and had become just another example of a vain ruler. All in all, the Swedish-Russian war made new information about the Ukraine available all over Europe, and sparked interest in the West among those wild people who lived somewhere in Russia, and, of course, Ivan Mazeppa became known for his strange role in the closing episode of that war.

As has been pointed out, however, the one book that contributed most to putting Mazeppa's story before the Western public was Voltaire's *Histoire de Charles XII*, first published in 1731; and the one event in it that is most important in Mazeppa's legend is his love intrigue with a Polish nobleman's wife that resulted in his banishment and wild ride across the

---

[8] According to John Robert Moore, *A Checklist of the Writings of Daniel Defoe* (Bloomington: Indiana University Press, 1960), pp. 126–27, 146–47, 175, Defoe published an ultraroyalist view of Charles XII in *A Short View of the Conduct of the King of Sweden* (London, 1717), which is a condensation and reworking of the 1715 version; and in 1720 he published an expanded version of the 1715 version . . . *with a Continuation to the Time of his* [Charles XII] *death*.

steppes tied naked to a horse. If Mazeppa's odd exile had been common knowledge among the Poles and Ukrainians before 1731, there was no published account of it before Voltaire's. The written sources for the banishment episode are the *Memoirs* (*1656–1688*) of Jan Pasek, a member of the Polish gentry, who recorded both facts and rumors about the Polish Court, and an anonymous account of the time, also in Polish; but both were unpublished until the nineteenth century. Pasek was a Polish writer who according to his *Memoirs* had in about 1663 been defeated by Mazeppa in a duel, which has led some historians to believe that Pasek made up the banishment incident as a slur on Mazeppa's character.

Voltaire, it should be noted, devotes only eight or ten paragraphs to Mazeppa in his *Histoire de Charles XII*. They take on an exaggerated importance in the context of the original work, because Byron set three of them off by citing them in the "Advertisement" to his *Mazeppa*. Furthermore, Voltaire's sources for the history of Charles XII were questioned by M. Nordberg, Charles XII's chaplain, and Voltaire subsequently explained in detail his sources without, however, giving his major sources: Henri de Limier's *Histoire de Suède sous la règne de Charles XII*. [9] The Ukrainian material could have come from a number of sources,[10] but none of them explains why Voltaire makes a point of supporting Ukrainian independence with Mazeppa as its chief spokesman. Borschak, however, pointed out that Voltaire's greatest source of information about the Ukraine and Mazeppa was probably Hetman Orlik's son.

Orlik, though not recognized as Hetman by Peter I, became Mazeppa's unauthorized successor and headed the first Mazeppist movement, an underground, quasi-revolutionary organization that operated in Eastern Europe and abroad to further Ukrainian independence. Orlik, using as an intermediary his son, then living in Paris, could have passed first-hand information about Mazeppa to Voltaire and impressed him with the cause of Ukrainian independence.[11]

Although Voltaire is sympathetic toward Mazeppa and the Ukraine in

[9] J. H. Brumfitt, *Voltaire: Historian* (London: Oxford University Press, 1958), p. 18.

[10] Eyewitness accounts by the French ambassadors to Sweden and Constantinople. Correspondence with King Leszczynski and Count Poniatowski. Kantemir's *Annales Turques*, Dalerai's *Anecdotes de Pologne*, La Mottraye's *Voyage en Europe, Asie et Afrique*, and Perry's *Étante présent de la Grande Russie*.

[11] Elie Borschak, "Histoire de l'Ukraine: Publication en Langue Ukranien parues dehors de l'U.S.S.R.," *Revue Historique*, 187 (1939): 278.

the *Histoire de Charles XII*, in the later *Histoire de la Russie sous la règne de Pierre le Grand* (1759) he recants and calls Mazeppa a traitor. The details of Mazeppa's life are the same in both histories, but the point of view is radically different. As Voltaire warns in the introduction ιο the *Histoire de la Russie*, "The History of Charles XII was amusing, that of Peter I is instructive." [12]

Voltaire's account of Mazeppa emphasizes the Hetman's strange arrival in the Ukraine, how his victories over the Turks gained him the confidence of the people, and how the Czar was obliged to make him Hetman: "His reputation grew day by day and obliged the Czar to make him Prince of the Ukraine." [13] Historically this is unsupported; Peter I was obliged to no one. But it probably served Orlik's purpose, as head of the Mazeppists, to establish Mazeppa's reputation as a powerful leader, and, perhaps more important, to assert the existence of a Ukrainian state that the Czar and his Polish subjects were doing their best to obliterate. The *Histoire de Charles XII* emphasizes the plight of a small nation struggling between two great powers, and as a result Mazeppa's reputation enlarges because he, the obvious underdog, suffered ordeals to become an emerging nation's leader, and then in the face of overwhelming odds he fought to make his countrymen free. Voltaire succeeds in sketching a small but intriguing prose portrait of the Hetman as a mysterious leader with an odd career.

Although Voltaire's *Histoire de Charles XII*, because of its international interpretation, initiated and helped to perpetuate the Mazeppa legend to great extent, that legend took sharper form in Western Europe a little later in a novel, *Memoires d'Azéma, contenant diverses anecdotes des règnes de Pierre le Grand, Empéreur de Russie et de l'Impératrice Catherine son Épouse*, translated from Russian by M. André Constant Dorville. The author clearly knew Voltaire's histories and the Mazeppa material therein; he used them for the general scheme of his novel, but amplified and fictionalized them enormously.

The number of editions and translations attests to the novel's popularity. It was first published in French in Amsterdam in 1764 with a second edition in 1766. In 1769 it was translated into Danish. A German trans-

---

[12] François Marie Arouet de Voltaire, *Oeuvres complètes de Voltaire* 52 vols. (Paris, 1877–85) 16:394.
[13] *Ibid.*, p. 237.

lation was completed in 1766 and reprinted in 1773. The book was not originally written in Russian, as the author asserts, but was translated from German into Russian; three editions appeared in Moscow between 1784 and 1796. Dorville seemed anxious to please the Russian Court with his novel by dedicating it to M. le Comte de Stroganoff, Chamberlain to the Russian Emperor. The image of Mazeppa that Dorville creates, however, is not at all the one the Russians held of him.

The author states in his introduction that the account was found among the papers of Stépanine, the child of Azéma and Mazeppa. Since there was no Azéma in Mazeppa's life and no Stépanine, the book is a fiction from the outset. Dorville uses that literary fashion, so usual in the eighteenth and early nineteenth centuries, of giving an air of reality to his fiction by writing a "true" account. What he has actually done in this case is to fictionalize Voltaire's already quasi-legendary account; the result is the creation of a completely legendary character only tenuously connected to historical fact.

The first half of the novel is devoted to Mazeppa's story. He was, according to Dorville, a Polish gentleman of an illustrious family. "In the usual troubles in Poland," [14] he lost his mother and father and was brought up by an uncle, Savieski, who, because of new political troubles (he sided with the liberty party), was forced to flee. Although Mazeppa was born a gentleman, the circumstances of his life forced him to work, for which he had been prepared by having had an aristocratic education. He became a page in Jean Casimir's Court, where he led a dissipated life but was still able to gain the King's confidence. At the Court Mazeppa is attracted to the beautiful Countess de Bra———. The Count, her husband, stages a ballet about Vulcan's Forge. "The Countess had the role of Venus, Mazeppa as Mars, and the prettiest women and most charming cavaliers made up the corps of gods and goddesses, while our old husband reserved for himself the role of Vulcan." [15] This is the classical tale of the old husband cuckolded by the young man. Mazeppa's youthful amorous escapades are balanced in later works about him by his car-

---

[14] André Constant Dorville, *Memoires d'Azéma, contenant diverses anecdotes des règnes de Pierre le Grand, Empéreur de Russie et de l'Impératrice Catherine son Épouse* (Amsterdam, 1764), p. 1. The translations are my own.

[15] *Ibid.*, p. 6.

rying-on in old age when he supposedly falls in love with the very young Maria Kochubey, his goddaughter.

The Polish Court is to go to Cracow. The Count proposes that he, the Countess, and Mazeppa stay at the *Château Bielastock*. The Count surprises Mazeppa at his wife's feet. In a fit of rage he stabs her, and Mazeppa turns on him, wounding him slightly. The Count decides to punish Mazeppa by having him tied naked to a wild horse and banishing him from Poland. What follows is the wild ride across the steppes, the psychological and physical effects of which are dramatically described. When the horse gets to the Ukraine with its burden, some peasants see it in the distance. The horse dies under Mazeppa and these peasants, who live near Baturyn (later to become Mazeppa's capital) rescue him. One of them addresses him in this manner:

From one side our harvests are preyed upon by the Moldaves, the Tartars from Budziak, and those from Precope; from the other our liberty, which we love more than life, is continually attacked by three great jailers: Muscovy, Turkey, and Poland. . . . One must name a protector, and we throw ourselves in the hands of the Poles. O my dear Mazeppa, you have confided in us your destiny. You were born among enemies, but you were unhappy. You are a man, and I am not afraid to let you read what is in my heart.[16]

What is in his heart is that Mazeppa is to deliver these lovers of liberty from the yoke of oppression; it seems that his destiny is to be their savior. As the author says, "The Cossacks may be in the fire, but they carry liberty in their hearts."

Mazeppa responds:

Exiled forever from my country, where cruel enemies judged my banishment, without comforts, without rank, and crushed me with sadness: those are the great things I can offer you for my fidelity. It is not the favors of fortune that bring men together; those chains are weak and break easily; only need joins men: if I can be useful to you and your appeals made me absolutely necessary, as in effect they do, then nothing could break the bonds that mutual interest will have forged.[17]

The old "peasant" who speaks to Mazeppa turns out to be his exiled uncle, Savieski. If Voltaire's remarks about Ukrainian independence are

---

[16] *Ibid.*, p. 18. [17] *Ibid.*, p. 22.

the source of these speeches, Dorville certainly has embroidered them. They illustrate well how Mazeppa's legend grew from the accumulation of detail around one episode in his life. Mazeppa the oddly found hero, the liberator, the oppressed Ukrainians, the spirit of freedom: all are there. Dorville adds a new twist by making Mazeppa Polish, then has him banished to become the liberator of a foreign country, not unlike those real and fictional freedom fighters of the late-eighteenth and the nineteenth centuries: Kosciuszko, Pulaski, Byron, von Steuben, O'Higgins, among others.

Mazeppa is taken to Baturyn, joins the army as an ordinary soldier, and rises in the ranks to become a general. His messiah-like arrival in the Ukraine is interpreted by the people as a sign of their coming freedom. While heading the army, Mazeppa learns that the Countess is alive in the Count's chateau. He returns there with his troops and kills the Count, but now the Countess has moral objections to their union. She dies in his arms, and his revenge has been foiled. He returns to the Ukraine to serve Peter I. Metima, a slave girl, falls madly in love with him, but he explains that he cannot love her because his experience with the Countess has chastened him, indicating a new fidelity to his "one" love. These episodes are purely from Dorville's imagination, but one can see that they add new psychological and sentimental dimensions to Mazeppa's character. He broods a good deal after the Countess's death.

In the midst of this melancholy, Peter I asks him to become Hetman of the Ukraine to protect it from the Swedes. Mazeppa agrees but for other reasons; the freedom of that country (harking back to the "peasant's" appeal) has never been out of his mind, and now is his first opportunity to act. He tells Peter at a banquet that the Ukraine should be independent; the Czar is furious at such a suggestion, and Mazeppa flees to save his life. He takes Azéma, a lady in Peter's Court, with him and goes to Metima for protection. At this point the secret treaty with Charles XII is mentioned in passing. Dorville does not interpret Mazeppa's secret alliance with Charles as traitorous. In fact, Mazeppa was also secretly negotiating with Poland at this time to oppose Peter I, but apparently Charles offered him better terms. Dorville does not mention the Polish negotiations, no doubt wanting to avoid having to explain Mazeppa's possible friendship with a country he supposedly hated. Dorville's attitude toward the Poles in this novel is somewhat ambiguous; he only hints at internal problems aggravated by Muscovy's grip on the country.

When Azéma and Mazeppa appear before Metima, she confesses that she was so blinded by her love for Mazeppa and his rejection of her that earlier she had betrayed him to the Czar. The ruse having been exposed, Mazeppa must confront Peter I, and the Battle of Poltava is fought. Peter wins, and Mazeppa and Azéma must flee to Bender, where the Hetman dies after a short illness. Azéma, a second woman Mazeppa evidently could love, goes on to other adventures, involving corsairs and English lords, in the rest of the novel.

Mazeppa emerges from this novel as an eighteenth-century courtier who, because he fell in love with the young wife of an elderly count, is banished and made to undergo great suffering. His deliverance from that ordeal includes his becoming a freedom fighter and for a brief time the leader of an emerging nation. The strange circumstances of his arrival in the Ukraine enhance his image as a savior among the people, especially among the peasants. He comes to value liberty because of his trial, which in turn fires his patriotism. It is important to note that he was not a patriot before his ordeal and that his banishment ultimately developed his latent patriotism. This change in character particularly fascinated Byron and Słowacki. Once his military greatness is developed, however, his passions reemerge, especially his desire for revenge. Its effects are a Pyrrhic victory: he kills the Count but loses the Countess. Mazeppa does not treat his outcome with objectivity or irony; he is overcome with sadness and a sense of fatalism, and his sentiments show themselves. "Mazeppa would have accepted his change of fortune courageously, but the tears of Azéma were a spectacle his sensibility could not sustain." [18]

Such feelings make him a likely candidate for a Romantic hero, that special kind of man who had already begun to make his appearance in literature: Werther, Mackenzie's man of feeling, Rousseau himself, René, and ultimately Childe Harold. Peter Thorslev in *The Byronic Hero* categorizes such men succinctly. Ivan Mazeppa is first of all a man with a flaw (his passions: love and revenge)—who tries to compensate for it through heroic action (fighting for Ukrainian independence). It happens that both his flaw and his heroism work toward his undoing. He does not really lament his fate; he feels more that life has conspired

[18] *Ibid.*, p. 122.

against him. Mazeppa, as described in Dorville's novel, has that odd combination of attributes that appealed to the Romantic imagination: sensitivity, passion, impulsiveness, thwarted good intentions, political engagement; in addition, there seemed to be something messianic about his political involvement. Although he blundered in his own life (and these blunders also affected his political mission) his personal life was subordinated to his political ideal. That he failed seems less important than that he tried so hard to achieve the ideal. Western Europe could respond imaginatively to such a man by the end of the eighteenth century.

At the same time Dorville's novel was being read and translated in Europe, two portraits of Mazeppa were painted by rather obscure Western artists. The first was done in 1775 by Jean Pierre Norbelin, a French artist who lived most of his life in Poland. *Mazepa Aetatis 70* [19] is the first extant posthumous portrait of the Hetman done by a man who never could have seen him. The portrait is probably an imaginative rendering of the Hetman based upon Norbelin's reading or upon the stories he may have heard about him. In the portrait Mazeppa appears as a typical eighteenth-century fop. His warrior qualities are suppressed in favor of his courtly ones. He seems a man of sensibility, softened, perhaps slightly decadent-looking to the twentieth-century viewer, but probably just a representative idea of a courtier for an eighteenth-century artist. After having read Dorville's novel, one sees a striking resemblance in Norbelin's portrait of Mazeppa, and though there is no direct evidence to support a claim for inspiration or influence from the novel, the suggestion is strong.

The other portrait, done later in the century, seems to have reached a wider European audience. It was painted by Daniel Beye, a German, from an engraving by Samuel Falk in 1796.[20] In one form or another it was published in Vienna, Budapest, Stockholm, and Warsaw between 1796 and 1835. In Beye's version, Mazeppa appears as an old man firmly holding in his right hand a mace, which rests on a table. His eyes and

---

[19] The best reproduction is in Bohdan Kentrschynskyi, *Mazepa* (Stockholm, 1962), p. 203. Alfred Jensen, *Mazepa: Historiska Bilder Från Ukraina och Karl XII:s Dager* (Lund, 1909), also has a reproduction, but it is of the engraving that appeared in the *Athenaeum*, Warsaw, 1842.

[20] It appears in both Jensen and Kentrschynski. In the latter it is a reproduction of the *Przyjaciel ludu* lithograph of 1835.

mouth seem to be smiling, but they also have a sinister quality; there is something Mephistophelian about his countenance. At a quick glance, one may get the impression from the way Mazeppa is holding the mace that he is actually holding a dagger. His face is thin, almost skeletal, almost as one would imagine one of Mrs. Radcliffe's villains. After continued examination, the possible duality in his character begins to flicker across one's mind.

These two pictorial representations are footnotes to the development of the Western European legend of Mazeppa and only indicate that Voltaire's and Dorville's shaping of the legend had already found form in other artists' works late in the eighteenth century. They did not popularize the works as much as the works that probably inspired them, nor did they serve as sources of influence as Byron's Oriental Tale *Mazeppa* did.

Mazeppa makes two more appearances in Western art before Byron's poem, and in them two important qualities of the legend are explored. Heinrich Bertuch, a public official in Gotha, published *Alexis Petrowitch: ein romantische-historische Trauerspiel in fünf Akten* in 1812 and Robert Etty anonymously published *The Cossack: A Poem*, in three cantos in London in 1815. Both works indicate that the interest in Mazeppa probably had deeper sources than a Romantic fascination with odd historical characters. The former shows the special way the Romantics often used history in their art, and the latter reminds one that there was an old tradition of the wild ride in European poetry. Both bear indirectly upon Byron's treatment of Mazeppa in that they signal ideas and trends already current while Byron was writing his poem.

Bertuch says he draws on some historical material in his play but informs his readers that he does not feel bound by history. He states that the play is an imaginative (*fantastische*) reworking of historical materials.[21] Whereas Dorville tried to persuade his readers of the truth of his account, Bertuch asserts that his point is to manipulate historical characters in a fictional situation to produce drama. Bertuch is doing to history what Schiller and Goethe, his Weimar colleagues, had done better in *Maria Stuarda* and *Egmont*. Behind all of this is the Romantic interpretation of Shakespeare's use of history in drama as understood by Wilhelm Schlegel. This little-known play does illustrate to some degree a shift in

---

[21] Heinrich Friedrich Christian Bertuch, *Alexis Petrowitch: en romantische-historische Trauerspiel in fünf Akten* (Gotha, 1812), pp. iv–v.

thinking about history between the eighteenth and nineteenth centuries. A set of loose historical associations and scattered historical facts were used to form the shell of drama that dealt with the spiritual and moral turmoil in one or more characters. The dramatic center of the play was personalized. It is as though one soliloquy from *Julius Caesar* were expanded into a five-act drama. The play often had a tenuous relation to history, which merely provided the setting, gave a general idea of a type of character—villain, robber, traitor, etc.—and may have established the direction of the action. Bertuch generally accepts Mazeppa as a subtly treacherous character who uses any means to undo his enemy, Peter I. The character is not, however, so simple as all that.

Bertuch makes Mazeppa a close friend of Alexis, Peter's son, whom the Czar had incarcerated and ultimately murdered in 1718 for, among other reasons, opposing his father's oppressive rule. Alexis is a weak, introverted character, and Mazeppa is his adviser as well as his friend, but he is not so close to the Czarevitch that he can tell him of the plan to murder Peter. In order not to give himself away, Mazeppa is forced to stab Alexis in the last scene. The life of a friend must be sacrificed for the greater cause: the freeing of the Ukrainian people from the Russian yoke. Mazeppa's anguish is caused by his need to reconcile the betrayal of his friend for the sake of Ukrainian independence. He makes long soliloquies about the ambiguity of life, about the difficulty a man has in making moral choices, about the defeat inherent in seeming victory. In short, Bertuch focuses on the Hetman's sensibilities. The final decision to kill Alexis is complicated by the Czarevitch himself. He has been mistrusted by his father all along, but when he learns Mazeppa's plan, he is overcome by filial feelings—a son cannot knowingly allow his father to be killed. Mazeppa is Alexis' close friend, but Peter I is a greater enemy: an enemy of the people. In order to salvage his plan, he must murder the Czarevitch before he tells his father. After the murder the troubled Mazeppa vanishes through a secret passage, while the Czar enters to see his dead son.

It is the morality in Mazeppa's action and the display of anguish in making moral choices that interest Bertuch, not the facts. He seems to want to point out the human difficulty of such choices and their often sad results. This play is certainly a highly fictional treatment of Mazeppa, which tries especially to show that it is not so easy to make distinctions between the patriot and the traitor, and Mazeppa evokes the dilemma well. The duality of character in Beye's painting seems to have been dramatically realized in Bertuch's play; both see a man with strong opposing forces in the Hetman's personality.[22]

Bertuch, then, as many Romantics, looked to history for examples of men and women who had to make a moral decision that often resulted in excruciating personal suffering, often anguish experienced secretly, inwardly, but undergone for some greater, idealistic cause, usually political or artistic. Such heroes, taken from history, appealed to the Romantic sensibility and appear in a plethora of Romantic works from the late eighteenth century in Germany to the middle of the nineteenth century in Russia.

Robert Etty's *The Cossack* had a different though significant relation to the Mazeppa legend. Etty's Cossack, Koustekoff, rides wildly through three cantos and meets Mazeppa briefly. Although there is no historical basis for this encounter, Koustekoff attends a birthday party for Mazeppa. Anticipating Byron's *Mazeppa*, I am struck by the similarity with which the Cossack's ride is described in both poems. The spirit of fury

[22] As a point of historical interest, I want to mention the allegation that a play, *Mazeppa, Hetman of the Ukraine*, was produced in Boston in March and April 1811, written by the Russian Consul to the United States, Aleksei Grigorevich Evstafiev. The allegation was made by I. V. Dubitsky, "Mazepa v zakhdnoevropeiskikh literaturakh," *Trizub* (October 17, 1937), pp. 15–18; repeated by Simon Demydekach, *Ukrainian Weekly* (November 11, 1944); reasserted by Maria Coleman, "Mazeppa, Traitor or 'Splendid Rebel,' " *Alliance Journal* 9 (1959): 21. Grace Overmyer, *America's First Hamlet* (New York: New York University Press, 1957), p. 406, says, "In 1812, seven years before the appearance of Byron's poem 'Mazeppa,' Payne had written to Alexie Eustaphieve, Russian Consul to the U.S. 'Returning Mazepa [sic]. Sorry to relinquish all prospects of appearing in Mazepa,' " citing the letters in the Luquer Collection. On the basis of Overmyer, Maria Coleman stated as a fact that this play existed, in her 1966 translation of Juliusz Słowacki's *Mazepa* into English. It is true that such a play was advertised in the *Boston Patriot* on April 24, 1812, and in the *Columbian Sentinel* in April. There is no sure way to know if such a play really exists, and if it does, who might be the author. In 1814, however, Evstafiev published in Boston *Reflections, Notes, and original Anecdotes celebrating the Character of Peter, the Great to which is added, a Tragedy in Five Acts entitled, "Alexis, the Czarewitz."* Nowhere in that volume is Mazeppa mentioned; yet, Evstafiev's play seems to be a reworking of Bertuch's with a few changes. Mazeppa seems to have been replaced by a character called the Confessor, a priest. He is an adviser to Alexis but is interested in preserving the power of the Church and not Ukrainian independence. The fifth act is changed so that Alexis dies of shock, the Confessor having been exposed as a sham in the fourth act. Perhaps the most one can say is that Evstafiev seems to have been deeply inspired by Bertuch's play. It may be that Evstafiev had Bertuch's play in mind when he wrote to Payne.

in the ride is also in Byron's poem: "And who are those on foaming steed,/ That scarce can follow with such speed?" (*Mazeppa*, I, 4–5). There is no reason to believe either that Byron did or did not read Etty's poem; however, I wonder if both were not in different ways responding to a larger theme that seemed so appealing to the European imagination: the wild ride on horseback. A reviewer of Byron's poem in 1819 said that he thought the source for Byron's *Mazeppa* was Cowper's poem "John Gilpin." [23] Although the review draws the wrong conclusions about the poem, it does point out that the theme of the wild ride was popular among English Romantics and earlier poets and probably emerged from the ballad tradition, permeating the imaginations of other European Romantics as well. The first major Polish, announced Romantic, poem, Antoni Malczewski's *Maria* (1825), uses the theme throughout, as does Adam Mickiewicz's *Farys* (St. Petersburg, 1829). It is also seen in many European Romantic paintings, especially those by Géricault, Delacroix, Fuseli, Stubbs, Gros, and Vernet. Etty's poem merely brings Mazeppa into juxtaposition with that older theme. The Polish theater historian Zbigniew Raszewski, writing about Mazeppa in nineteenth-century painting, makes an observation that helps to explain why the Romantics perhaps responded so enthusiastically to the Mazeppa theme, and by extension suggests that Mazeppa's ordeal on horseback may be only an addition to an older, simpler theme:

Beginning in the Romantic era, Mazeppa enjoyed a meaningful sympathy in the West as the leader of the exotic but unfortunate Ukrainians. However, he would not have gained such popularity if a strange fate were not attached to his name. From some forgotten past, European art was interested in the hero in shackles already tied to a horse or dragged (or carried) by a horse. From these paintings (Jung would say: from these two archetypes) the Romantics especially admired the second. [24]

So then, Mazeppa's image in Western Europe already had a fairly defined legendary aura before Byron wrote his poem in 1819, and the legend incorporated many characteristics that would appeal to the Romantics. The historical circumstances of Mazeppa's life were generally passed over in the West, and upon a few facts and what seems to be a

---

[23] William Maginn, "John Gilpin and Mazeppa," *Blackwoods Magazine* 5 (1819): 434–39.

[24] Zbigniew Raszewski, "Mazepa," *Prace o literaturze i teatrze ofiarowane Zygmuntowi Szweykowskiemu* (Wrocław, 1966), p. 437.

good deal of rumor a legendary type took form. The two major artistic treatments of Mazeppa before Byron, Dorville's and Bertuch's, emphasize his sensitivity. According to them, he is a strong man, sometimes ruthless, but his heart is moved by love and friendship. He is passionate and courageous, but when he acts emotionally the outcome is unsatisfactory. He is a great man whose heroism is undermined by his human flaws, which themselves very often seem noble. Like so many of the heroes of the Romantic age, his heroism is *manqué*.

Byron managed to bring these elements together in a more meaningful way, a way that would rejuvenate the treatment of Mazeppa during the next thirty years.

2.

BYRON'S MAZEPPA

LORD BYRON'S *Mazeppa*, his last Oriental Tale, is a little-known poem, part of whose obscurity is due to its having been written after *Childe Harold*, Canto IV and before *Don Juan*, Cantos I and II, works of such importance and brilliance that they tend to make a good deal of Byron's other poetry dim by comparison. When *Mazeppa* is critically discussed, generally it is regarded as a serioironic, transitional poem in which Byron mixes his old-style hero—Conrad, Lara, Manfred, Harold—with his new, ironic hero, Don Juan. Wedged as the poem is between those two larger works so disparate in tone, *Mazeppa* has become for some critics a modulation in Byron's work from Romantic egotism to Romantic irony, as a poem "between" poems, significant primarily in the light of other poems.[1] Neither Byron nor his friends seem to have given it much consideration, although *Mazeppa* received about as many reviews on its publication as did the first two cantos of *Don Juan*.

Byron's *Mazeppa* is, however, extremely important in the further development of the Hetman's legend in Europe during the Romantic period. The poem takes up the themes of history, leadership, love, freedom, and death as they relate to Mazeppa's life and indicate something of Byron's feelings about them in 1818–19. The center of the poem is Mazeppa's fantastic ride, as told by the aging Hetman himself the evening after his defeat at the Battle of Poltava. Byron, however, does not merely describe the ride and elaborate upon the details in Voltaire's *Histoire de Charles XII* and Dorville's *Memoires d'Azéma*, but tries to render the ride and Mazeppa's experiences during it symbolically. Such a treat-

---

[1] D. Englaender, *Lord Byrons Mazeppa: Eine Studie* (Berlin, 1897), p. 59; William Calvert, *Byron: Romantic Paradox* (New York: Russell & Russell, 1962), pp. 131–32; Leslie Marchand, *Byron's Poetry: A Critical Introduction* (Boston: Houghton Mifflin, 1965), pp. 70–71.

ment of the theme raises the legend to a new level that serves as a source of inspiration for later Eastern and Western Romantic artists.

The genesis of *Mazeppa* is not a clear and simple story, for Byron said little about the poem. The two poems of this period that do shed some light on *Mazeppa* are what Byron called the "not very intelligible" "Ode on Venice," and the earlier "Prisoner of Chillon." There is, of course, ample historical, literary, and biographical material available to show that Byron could have known about and had information about the Hetman, but there is no explicit reason, according to the evidence, why Byron should write about Mazeppa at all, especially as he was in the middle of his "Italian Period." [2]

Byron's list of books, compiled in 1807, indicates that he was evidently already well informed about Eastern Europe,[3] and, as Albert Tezla has demonstrated, Byron was reading and learning about the East continually from his youth until his death.[4] He seems, however, to have become more interested in using subjects from the Slavic East after *Mazeppa* was published, for a large section of *Don Juan* is set in Russia, and the *Age of Bronze* includes a good deal of material about Russia related to the Congress of Verona. Furthermore, both poems deal knowledgeably with Russia's history and culture.

For most critics Byron's particular source of inspiration and information is obvious: Voltaire's *Histoire de Charles XII*. The "Advertisement" to

---

[2] There is an interesting theory that came out of Poland late in the nineteenth century (see Michał Modzelewski's letter in *Kurjer Warszawski*, 1873, no. 108) and was reiterated recently. Antoni Malczewski, the Polish-Ukrainian poet of the early nineteenth century, supposedly met Byron in Venice in 1817. They were to have become friends. Both poets were supposed to have discussed Polish subjects and in particular Mazeppa, in whom Byron became so fascinated that he wrote a poem about the Hetman. Malczewski could have met Byron at a Venetian *conversazione* and could have talked about these things with the Englishman. Byron, however, does not allude to Malczewski or to any encounter the two might have had, much less to a friendship, in any of the biographical material available. Also, Malczewski has not documented his meetings or meeting with Byron; this information was passed by word of mouth to friends. Jozef Ujejski, *Antoni Malczewski: poeta i poemat* (Warsaw, 1921), pp. 83–84; Marian Moore Coleman, *Mazeppa: Polish and American* (Cheshire, Conn.: Cherry Hill Books, 1966), p. 56. Alfred Jensen also repeats the story in *Mazeppa* (Lund, 1909), pp. 299–300.

[3] Thomas Moore, *The Works of Lord Byron: With His Letters and Journals and His Life* (London, 1832), pp. 46–47.

[4] Albert Tezla, "Byron's Oriental Tales: A Critical Study" (Diss., Univ. of Chicago, 1953), ch. I.

the poem cites three passages from that book; even page numbers are given. Their argument is strengthened by a letter to Hobhouse on March 31, 1818, in which Byron wrote that he had just bought a complete set of Voltaire's works in Venice.[5] Although Byron refers specifically to the *Histoire*, he most certainly also read Voltaire's *Histoire de la Russie sous la règne de Pierre le Grand*, which is a companion volume to the *Histoire de Charles XII* in most sets of Voltaire's works, but in which Voltaire changed his mind about the Hetman, seeing him as a traitor to Peter I. Byron was a great admirer of Peter I, and surely Voltaire's changed view of Mazeppa affected his own view of the Hetman. Byron is obviously aware of the flaws in Mazeppa's character, which he develops with an eye to the Hetman's betrayal of friendship and trust.[6]

Byron's choosing to write a poem about a historical figure and pointing to a historical source is not at all unusual. He was always interested in history, always read a great many historical works, and came to feel more than ever about the time he was writing *Mazeppa* that historical fact was essential to the foundation of his poetry. There have been critics who have theorized about Byron's use of and attitude toward history in this and other works, but I tend to agree with Graham Hough that Byron did not apply any rigid theory of history in his work though he had a reverence for historical fact.[7] His remarks in a letter of April 2, 1817, indicate the special importance of facts to him.

There is still in the Doge's palace, the black veil painted over Faliero's picture, and the staircase whereon he was first crowned Doge, and subsequently decapitated. This was the thing that most struck my imagination in Venice—more than the Rialto, which I visited for the sake of Shylock; and more, too, than Schiller's "Armenian," a novel which took great hold of me when a boy. It is also called the "Ghost Seer," and I never walked down St. Marks by moonlight without thinking of it, and *"at nine o'clock he died."*—But I hate things *all fiction;* and therefore the *Merchant [of Venice]* and *Othello* have no great association to me but *Pierre* has. There should always be some foundation of fact for the most airy fabric, and pure invention is but the talent of the liar.[8]

    [5] Leslie Marchand, *Byron: a Biography*, 3 vols. (New York: Knopf, 1957), 2:687.
    [6] Cf. ch. IV of the *Histoire de Charles XII* and chs. XVII and XVIII, Part I, in the *Histoire de la Russie sous la règne de Pierre le Grand*.
    [7] See the first chapter of the diss. (Univ. of No. Carolina, 1954) by Orville White, "Lord Byron's Use and Conception of History"; Graham Hough, *Image and Experience* (Lincoln: University of Nebraska Press, 1960), p. 136.
    [8] Peter Quennel, *Byron: a Self Portrait*, 2 vols. (New York: Scribner's, 1950) 2:404–5.

Beginning with the *Siege of Corinth* and *Parisina* in 1815, Byron grounded more and more of his work in historical fact, and by the time he wrote *Mazeppa* he was probably under the spell of some of Voltaire's ideas, especially those in the "Discourse on the History of Charles XII."

Voltaire's *Histoire* was meant to teach princes that ambition even in the best of men is doomed, and he stressed this idea by extracting it from the facts. *Mazeppa* is in part a study of ambition among rulers and how their victories turned into defeats. Instead of considering this idea from the point of view of Charles XII or Peter I, Byron chose to analyze it in the least-well-known of the three, the one who dared the most and who lost his one great gamble on the day of the Battle of Poltava.

From the outset one of Byron's major themes in *Mazeppa* is the leadership of a nation by a ruler, and to make his point he compares, in different degrees, Napoleon, Charles XII, Mazeppa, Jean Casimir, and the Palatine, the wronged husband. In the first section of the poem Byron draws a parallel between Charles XII and Napoleon, because both were defeated by a "triumphant czar" and "Moscow's walls were safe again." [9] These two men were defeated by the same nation almost one hundred years apart; perhaps, the poem suggests, there are analogies to be drawn, and lessons to be learned. Pushkin draws the same comparison in his "Introduction" to *Poltava* in 1829. In the first section one learns that 1812 was a "more memorable year" than 1709. In fact, according to the narrator, all that happened between Napoleon and Russia was more memorable than what transpired between Charles XII and Russia.

> Until a day more dark and drear,
> And a more memorable year,
> Should give to slaughter and to shame
> A mightier host and a haughtier name;
> A greater wreck, a deeper fall,
> A shock to one—a thunderbolt to all.

$$(I, 9-14)$$

History seems to be repeating itself but producing more devastating results. Without concluding his comments, the narrator shifts the subject

---

[9] All citations of Byron's *Mazeppa*, *Ode on Venice*, and *Prisoner of Chillon* are from *The Complete Poetical Works of Byron*, ed. Paul E. More (Boston: Houghton Mifflin, 1935), pp. 406–15, 452–55, 402–6.

to Charles XII and how he "was taught to fly." Before the Battle of Poltava, he had not experienced military defeat. The narrator makes clear
that Charles XII is to be identified with ambition: "And not a voice was
heard t'upbraid/Ambition in his humbled hour." He is the personifica-
tion of it. When ambition is humbled, when truth need no longer fear
power, even then no one revolts against Charles XII: he still commands
and leads his men who remain loyal and aid his escape. One reason why
the Gieta episode, the second quotation from *Histoire de Charles XII* in the
"Advertisement," is introduced at this point ("His [Charles XII] horse
was slain, and Gieta gave/ His own—and dies the Russians' slave") is to
show the extent of this man's loyalty to his King. The King is made to
rest under a tree while the enemy threatens the encampment. The narrator asks: "Are these the laurels and repose/ For which the nations strain
their strength?" In other words, is this the outcome of war? And because
Charles's defeat prompts the question, is this then the outcome of ambition? The narrator does not berate Charles in his misery; in fact, he ad-
mires him for his ability to bear defeat well: "Kinglike the monarch bore
his fall," but the reader remembers that Charles did fall. Not only is
Charles noble, but he also has great self-control: he reacts to his pain
with Stoic silence.

Section III begins by describing the King surrounded by his few men
and their horses and how all—men and animals—seem to become equal
when danger threatens: "For danger levels man and brute,/ And all are
fellows in their need." The first two sections are devoted to Charles XII,
and do more than merely set the scene; almost immediately the character
and career of the Swedish monarch come under analysis and historical
analogies are drawn. Were this all the space devoted to Charles in the
poem, Byron would have already reiterated Voltaire's opinion of him,
but Byron extends his analysis further and includes other rulers.

Mazeppa is introduced in section III and the action focuses on his taking care of his horse. Charles, who speaks for the first time in the poem,
compliments Mazeppa for being such a good horseman. The King compares Mazeppa to Alexander the Great, a magnanimous gesture on
Charles's part because he liked to compare himself to Alexander. Charles
prevails upon Mazeppa to tell the story of how he became such a fine
horseman, and Mazeppa begins to explain what his life was like as a page

in the court of Jean Casimir fifty years before. During his personal narrative Mazeppa draws direct parallels between the Swedish monarch and the Polish one.

> A learned monarch, faith! was he,
> And most unlike your majesty:
> He made no wars, and did not gain
> New realms to lose them back again;
> And (save debates in Warsaw's diet)
> He reign'd in most unseemly quiet
> Not that he had no cares to vex,
> He loved the masses and their sex;
> And sometimes these so froward are,
> They made him with himself at war;
> But soon his wrath being o'er, he took
> Another mistress, or new book.
>
> (IV, 131–42)

The amusing and ironic tone does not conceal the criticism levelled against Charles; the great wit and cunning of Mazeppa make him realize that probably only in this manner—with a wry smile—can he make such criticisms palatable to the Swedish monarch, defeated in battle for the first time that morning. Charles waged war deliberately: he was acutely ambitious; and now it was apparent that he had fought so long and hard only to lose. Casimir, on the other hand, was a courtier, as Mazeppa describes him, most interested in literature and ladies. But then Mazeppa led a country, too. And Jean Casimir's propensity for women was not unlike his own, yet Casimir had a successful reign. Jean Casimir seemed to surpass both Charles and Mazeppa because he never waged war.

The next step in Byron's analysis of leadership is for Mazeppa to show how his life as a leader reflects what he has already said about Charles and Jean Casimir. Mazeppa is like Casimir in his passionate love for women. In sections IV, V, and VI, Mazeppa has related the story of his affair with the young Theresa and how her husband, the old Palatine, decided to send him into exile lashed to a wild horse. Of course the Palatine is Mazeppa's archenemy because he separates the two lovers, but the characteristics of the Palatine that Mazeppa chooses to speak about are his political ambition and his personal vanity: both reflect upon Charles's own character, both are involved in his defeat.

In the next section Mazeppa indulges in some precise self-criticism that ultimately, however, points up Charles's shortcomings. Throughout this analysis Mazeppa criticizes his and other rulers' successes in leading men and nations by linking them to these men's passionate natures or their lack of passion. But then Mazeppa impulsively asserts that the outcome is the same whether a man be a lover or a celibate.

> I loved, and was beloved again—
> They tell me, Sire, you never knew
> Those gentle frailties; if 't is true,
> I shorten all my joy or pain;
> To you 't would seem absurd or vain.
> But all men are not born to reign,
> Or o'er their passion, or as you,
> Thus o'er themselves and nations too.
> I am—or rather *was*—a prince,
> A chief of thousands, and could lead
> Them on where each would foremost bleed;
> But could not o'er myself evince
> The like control.
>
> (V, 282–94)

Mazeppa argues from the point of view of love, of his great passion, of his indulgence; but in spite of the obviously debilitating power of his passion, still he did become a prince, he did lead men, and he ruled too. Mazeppa finally cries out:

> —I'd give
> The Ukraine back again to live
> It o'er once again.
>
> (V, 304–6)

The implication is that it is better to love and fight and to have lost, both women and wars, than not to have loved at all. The final thrust is at Charles's celibacy. Mazeppa asserts his joy of living, loving, ruling, and even warring, for in them is his greatest glory.

Byron is not necessarily espousing such a view but is letting the irony and cynicism emerge by letting the Hetman "explain" himself. Charles XII does not reply. The implication of those lines is that any personal political ambition in a leader, whether couched in seeming virtues or vices, leads to war and defeat. One recalls that the poem began by referring to Napoleon, a perfect example of such ambition, especially from Byron's point of view.

Byron, through his narrator and Mazeppa, does establish the greatness of Charles XII as a ruler and leader of men, while pointing out the extent of his ambition and stressing the immediacy of his defeat. Byron does not reach any cause-and-effect conclusions; he merely presents the reader with a comparison of two rulers who had opposing temperaments and very different experiences, but who came to the same defeat. Voltaire wrote his *Histoire de Charles XII* to teach princes a lesson, but to Byron it seemed that history still had not taught man the futility of ambition.

Although Byron was influenced by Voltaire's views of Mazeppa and ideas of history in the general way described, it seems that Byron's citations from the *Histoire de Charles XII* are incidental to *Mazeppa*, though Voltaire's ideas are not, and that the poem may have some other source.[10] In an early edition of Byron's works edited by George Clinton is the following note: "A French novel, called 'D'Azhema,' is another of the sources from which Lord Byron took some of the incidents of his tale [*Mazeppa*]: the ground work of the story seems, however, to be quite true."[11] That is André Dorville's novel the *Memoires d'Azéma*. In his letter of April 2, 1817, Byron speaks about facts but implies that he is not averse to fiction either: the "most airy fabric" must always be *grounded* in fact. Dorville's novel fits this description well, and it has similarities to *Mazeppa*. Resemblances are so close that I am convinced that Byron must have used it extensively, even though there is no evidence that he read or owned the novel.

First, the outlines of the biography that Mazeppa tells in Byron's poem are spelled out in the same way in the novel, especially what he says about Theresa and her old husband the Palatine; in the original they are the Count and Countess de Bra——. Byron does alter the situation a little:

> But one fair night, some lurking spies
> Surprised and seized us both.

[10] I was struck by the arguments of Lydia Holubnycky in a recently published article, "Mazeppa in Byron's Poem and History," *The Ukrainian Quarterly* 15, no. 4, pp. 336–45, where she shows that much of the historical detail could not have come from Voltaire. I disagree, however, with her conclusion that Byron used Jan Pasek's *Memoirs* as a major source, for they were not published until 1836, and then in Polish, making them doubly inaccessible to Byron.

[11] George Clinton, Esq., *Memoire of the Life and Writing of Lord Byron* (London, 1831), p. 413.

> The Count was something more than wroth;
> I was unarm'd; but if in steel,
> All cap-a-pie from head to heel,
> What 'gainst their number could I do?—
> 'Twas near his castle, far away
> From city or from succor near,
> And almost on the break of day.
> I did not think to see another,
> My moments seem'd reduced to few;
> And with one prayer to Mary Mother,
> And, it may be, a saint or two,
> As I resign'd me to my fate,
> They led me to the castle gate:
> Theresa's doom I never knew.
>
> (VIII, 325–40)

He eliminated the melodrama of the stabbings, but the rest is much the same: the castle at Bialystock away from the city; the lovers caught together; the disappearance of the Countess; and Mazeppa's punishment. In the novel Mazeppa finally returns to raze the Count's castle and kill him. Byron's Mazeppa executes the same revenge, except that no mention is made of the Palatine's fate:

> I would fain
> Have paid their insult back again.
> I paid it well in after days:
> There is not a castle gate. . . .
>
> (X, 391ff)

Whereas Dorville dramatizes the situation and has Mazeppa kill the Count, Byron simply chooses to describe the razing of the castle. Also, there is no confrontation of Mazeppa with Theresa in *Mazeppa*, but in section VI Mazeppa's love for Theresa is as passionate and special as that described in the novel. Byron probably did not like the melodramatic situations in the *Memoires* or the overly sentimental hero; he was able to pass over them by having his Mazeppa an old man looking back on his youth and recalling it with ironic compassion, and with an eye to censoring from it what was ignoble. Mazeppa, as any man, would no doubt present his life in its best light. Or, perhaps Byron was willing to follow Dorville as far as the details that contradict Voltaire, simply omitting what seemed unhistorical.

Byron's description of the wild ride may be an amplification of Dorville's.

Naked, Mazeppa was carried by the savage beast across mud and precipices. His attempts to get loose only served to goad the animal's fury and that of the unfortunate burden it carried. Mazeppa, stretched and bleeding, his body covered with rope burns is led into the Ukraine, twenty-four leagues from Poland. Undoubtedly, he was in a deep faint, for when he came to, he found himself on the banks of the Boristhenes in the hands of some peasants who were trying to help him.[12]

To be sure, Byron has his Mazeppa wake in the hut of a Cossack maiden, but that seems the only difference. This description could be the working outline for the center of his poem.

Most convincing, however, are the final remarks about Mazeppa in the novel, they are made by the narrator.

What a sad chain of misfortunes linked Mazeppa's days. I recall them painfully! Born of parents in the first ranks of the Polish Court, he was plunged into the most awful misery because of unforseen events. He was abandoned. One pure day seemed to illuminate his youth; a love intrigue almost cost him his life because of an unheard-of punishment. *But who can read the decrees of providence?* This vengeance exercised against him was the route that led him to honours. He became the master of the same people he had implored for help earlier. During his good fortune the arms of assassins were always leveled at him. One more step, and he would have freed his country from the yoke of the Muscovites. One moment destroyed such well founded hopes. The Battle of Poltava was the end of his good fortune. The blood that ran from a deep and dangerous wound drained his energy, and soon ended his agitated days. He fled with the heroes who for nine years had made tombs in the North and who were interred themselves in the profound abysses into which fate drew them.[13]

This passage should be compared to what Byron says in X, 407–22 and XX, 848–54. Mazeppa's "What mortal his own doom may guess?" seems very close to the underlined sentence above. In the sections of *Mazeppa* cited, Byron seems to have put many of the words, in translation, into the mouth of his Mazeppa.

Dorville's novel probably played a large part in the genesis of *Mazeppa*,

---

[12] Constant André Dorville, *Memoires d'Azéma, contenant diverses ancedotes des règnes de Pierre le Grand, Empéreur de Russie et de l'Impératrice Catherine son Épouse* (Amsterdam 1764), pp. 14–15.

[13] *Ibid.*, pp. 121–22. My emphasis.

even though neither Byron nor his circle refer to it. It may in part explain how in the midst of all the Italian poems a Slavic one surfaced. Had he found it on some bookshelf in an Italian villa? Had some Polish *émigré* passed it to him? Somehow the novel must have reached him. Was the Venetian Consul's secretary, a Mr. Dorville, who knew Byron fairly well, a relative of Dorville or a possessor of the novel? Of course Byron's treatment of the theme is original, and he did want to emphasize its historical basis, hence the quotations from Voltaire; yet on one level the poem turns out to be a curious mixture of fact and fiction. He seems to be taking the outlines of Dorville's fiction, recasting it into a new mold, and filling out an essentially melodramatic character and situations with historical facts and ideas. Byron is himself adding to the Mazeppa legend, while his predecessors' works provided the facts and psychological construct of his main character. *Mazeppa* then is the third clear stage in the development of the Hetman's Western legend: Voltaire's initial bringing together of some fact and hearsay, then Dorville's amplification of Voltaire, and finally Byron's reworking of both.

Yet Byron only used the historical and legendary elements to frame the center of his poem. As Albert Tezla pointed out recently, the literary frame of some of Byron's tales is historical and is there to set the story on its way quickly; [14] this is how *Mazeppa* seems structured, too. The historical material in *Mazeppa* acts as a gateway to a central subject, theme, or character. If such a frame is not to appear artificial and merely a literary device to get to the main subject, it must be integral with or reflect or complement the main subject, perhaps even be analogous to it. The theme that holds the central subject securely in its frame—Mazeppa's ride and near death while strapped naked to a horse—is personal, public, and historical defeat. Defeat is, of course, closely allied to the opening theme of leadership, although only a negative aspect of it. According to Byron, any leader corrupted by ambition will be defeated. The defeat of Charles XII (and Mazeppa) at Poltava; Mazeppa's unsuccessful love affair that brings temporary glory as Hetman of the Ukraine but ends in defeat; his losing Theresa, the Hetmanship, and his best men, and his dying in a few months in exile in Turkey; the defeat of Sweden; the Palatine's defeat; Napoleon's defeat—all echo one another and reinforce

---

[14] Tezla, p. 130.

one another. This theme provides the poem with its coherence while affording frame and background for the most significant episode of the tale.

That center is Mazeppa and the circumstances of his ride, and it is extremely difficult to separate the two, for the character becomes the action and his action becomes totally identifiable with Mazeppa. Robert Escarpit's observations about Mazeppa are therefore not so surprising, though he seems not able to explain precisely Mazeppa's uniqueness. "It would be difficult to reconcile Mazeppa with the image of the traditional Byronic heroes. This grand old man has nothing of the fatal man. He is calm, quiet, attentive, but amusing and good. He is an old campaigner, full of practical sense and thoughtful authority." [15] Tezla sharpens the focus when he says that "Mazeppa is motivated by the same basic passions as the other heroes, by love and hate, but is not so violent and evil that he is set inevitably apart from moral action and the influence of finer feelings in human nature." [16] There are traces of great passion in Mazeppa; and he does possess a certain kinship to Byron's Noble Outlaws.

Using Thorslev's classification of Byronic heroes, Mazeppa is most like the Noble Outlaw, though Thorslev does not classify Mazeppa at all. "He [the Noble Outlaw] is figured as having been wronged either by intimate personal friends, or by society in general, and his rebellion is thus always given a plausible motive." [17] Mazeppa's crime is that he has stolen the heart of a young Polish countess. He is an adulterer, but plausibly so, for the Countess's husband is an unpleasant old man. Mazeppa's punishment is his wild ride, but that seems too severe. To compensate for his gross punishment, he seems to have a double revenge: he becomes Hetman of the Ukraine which, in turn, enables him to return to the Palatine's castle and raze it. But his revenge is undercut because Theresa never returns to him, and at the opening of the poem he has been deposed as Hetman. He bears all these burdens sternly, and his streak of vengeance only occasionally surfaces in the poem. His life, as Englaender pointed out, is a cycle of crime and punishment. [18]

---

[15] Robert Escarpit, *Lord Byron: un tempérament littéraire* (Paris, 1955), p. 215.

[16] Tezla, p. 209.

[17] Peter L. Thorslev, *The Byronic Hero: Types and Prototypes* (Minneapolis: University of Minnesota Press, 1962), p. 69.

[18] Englaender, p. 11.

Mazeppa is noble in both senses of the word; he is titled and magnanimous, and Thorslev's description of the Noble Outlaw can therefore
apply to him: "In all of his appearances the Noble Outlaw personified
the Romantic nostalgia for the days of personal heroism, for the age
when it was still possible for a leader to dominate his group of followers
by sheer physical courage, strength of will, and personal magnetism." [19]
Mazeppa has all the qualities of this kind of Byronic hero, but they are
not so pronounced or so intense as in other illustrations of this type. As
he turns out, Mazeppa is one of Byron's most realistic creations, heroic
within the bounds of human potential, almost forced to the heroic by the
circumstances of his life, but not somehow by nature destined to be a
hero. Mazeppa is trapped in apparently a hopeless situation, but like
other Byronic heroes—e.g., Bonnivard, Tasso, and Don Juan in Canto
II—he survives with a desperate commonsense endurance. He is not
seeking self-destruction. Mazeppa is a *menschliche* or *allzumenschliche*
hero, to borrow these terms from Thorslev; [20] he is not Conrad or Prometheus, though they do come to mind for a moment when one considers Mazeppa's incredible ordeal; yet he remains less grand and more
human.

At no time, not even during and after Mazeppa's great ordeal, does
one feel that Mazeppa is anything but a human being, a fine specimen of
a man. He loves hard and daringly, possesses great physical strength; his
defeat and his gestures of hope, especially at seventy, strongly underline
his human nature. In a more general way, that Mazeppa is an actual historical figure reinforces his earthliness. Byron goes to great lengths to
describe the physical quality of Mazeppa's experience of death-in-life,
which has overtones of metaphysical and aesthetic meaning for other artists, but which for Byron is grounded in the real world of accurate phys-
iological and psychological detail. With all the emphasis on the physical,
the man and his experience still become greater than themselves.

Byron has given almost as much attention to the horse that carries
Mazeppa as to the hero. The fury of the horse's ride across the plain and
his death are described in detail. What seem to be emphasized are his
speed, his implacable sense of wanting to return to the land of his
origin—the Ukraine—and his death once he got there. Mazeppa is

---

[19] Thorslev, p. 69.   [20] *Ibid.*, p. 92.

strapped to this horse and his ordeal of almost dying—and Byron is most explicit here—is related to the horse's experience and death.

In the third section, when Mazeppa is introduced into the poem, one notices that Byron describes extensively Mazeppa's care of the horse he has ridden in the Battle of Poltava. The horse, "shaggy and swift, and strong of limb," is devoted to his master. Mazeppa treats him as though he might be another human being. Such attention to the horse seems to signify a number of ideas: most generally, it establishes Mazeppa as a sympathetic character, who has been not made callous by years of warfare, and who, even in extreme circumstances, keeps a level head and is thoughtful to his beast. But more particularly, Mazeppa was saved by a horse—as one learns in the tale he tells in later sections—so his respect for and interest in horses may also be a natural result of that experience. In section II the narrator introduces the example of Gieta, who gave his horse to save his King. In Charles's case, as in Mazeppa's, a horse plays an important role in saving his life. Also at this point, the mutual loyalty of Mazeppa and his horse parallels the loyalty of Mazeppa and the men to Charles XII. An explicit relation between man and horse is made when Charles says in section II that King, men, and horse become equal in the throes of danger. Such is one aspect of the reader's introduction to the poem—part of his preliminary conditioning, so to speak—to understanding the significance of that other horse: that one that sped Mazeppa to safety fifty years before.

Most of section IX is devoted to a description of that horse: ". . . he was a noble steed,/ A Tartar of the Ukrainian breed. . . ." He was "wild," "untaught," and " 'Twas but a day he had been caught." How aptly these words also apply to Mazeppa, who had just been caught by the Palatine and also was in a fury. Two furious animals, both trapped in different ways, are tied to one another. As each lives out his destiny— the horse to die and Mazeppa to be saved—one realizes that the fate of one not only reflects the other, but is also necessary to the fate of the other. In other words, the horse's return to the Ukraine, to his homeland, to die reinforces by analogy Mazeppa's ordeal of almost dying and points up the bringing of Mazeppa to a land of which he is eventually to become the Hetman. The homeland of one becomes the homeland of the other. Now perhaps one can see that the sacrifice of the horse's life becomes the new source of Mazeppa's life. Tying the man to the beast seems to be a way of concretely demonstrating how alike and related they are.

One is likely to miss these parallels even when reading the poem very carefully, because Byron emphasized so strongly the swiftness and fury of the ride. But even in section X, where the wild ride begins, one sees that Byron is surely drawing the reader's attention to parallels here, too. Soon after the ride's commencement, he introduces a digression by Mazeppa on the subject of revenge. He says earlier in the section: "With sudden wrath I wrench'd my head,/ And snapp'd the cord . . ." to show the strength of his anger. Then follows his description of the ultimate destruction of the Palatine's castle. The section ends with these lines:

> For time at last sets all things even—
> And if we do but watch the hour,
> There never yet was human power
> Which could evade, if unforgiven,
> The patient search and vigil long
> Of him who treasures up a wrong.
>
> (X, 417–22)

The speed and wrath of the horse imply Mazeppa's relentless pursuit of revenge and the fury with which he achieved it. What Byron has done with the ride in this case is to juxtapose it to Mazeppa's feelings of revenge and sense of satisfaction. Just as Mazeppa's revenge was expended in razing the castle, so too will the horse's fury be expended in his death: the animal's fury is analogous to the man's state of being.

The next section begins "Away, away, my steed and I,/ Upon the pinions of the wind,/ All human dwellings left behind"; the speed and fury will be put to other uses now to help to develop other themes in the poem. For instance, in section XI what is pointed up is the intimate relation between the action of the horse and Mazeppa.

> . . . my bound and slender frame
> Was nothing to his angry might,
> And merely like a spur became.
> Each motion which I made to free
> My swoln limbs from their agony
> Increased his fury and afright:
> I tried my voice, —'t was faint and low,

> But yet he swerved as from a blow;
> And, starting to each accent, sprang
> As from a sudden trumpet's clang.
>
>   (XI; 450–59)

What seems most important in this struggle is that the horse's freedom apparently produces Mazeppa's pain and vice versa, so that Mazeppa's life seems bound to the horse's death. Perhaps here the metaphor is explicit: the horse is Mazeppa and vice versa; the one's death equals the other's life. Byron makes this intense identification through most of the poem, trying apparently to fuse the parts of the analogy so that Mazeppa's ride might become, in modern terms, a symbol.

In section XII, Byron returns to a simple description of the horse's swiftness after introducing the wolves that pursue them. In this instance the ride seems to serve the purely narrative purpose of showing the passage of time, and what predominates is the landscape in which the action of the ride takes place. One must go back for a moment to see how Byron has used the landscape and setting to this point, for they serve as the backdrop in this central section. In section II, Charles XII and his company come to rest and make camp in a place surrounded by the enemy. "They laid him [Charles] by a savage tree,/ In outworn nature's agony. . . ." In other words, this place is analogous to the King's physical and mental state of being, and in general Byron will use the setting to reflect his characters in this way. In section XI Mazeppa leaves "All human dwelling . . . behind." Byron has set the ride and the death-in-life experience in nature, beyond the bounds of civilization in which man is isolated. In the previous section, where the ride began, Mazeppa has left all human sound behind. Boundless wild woods and plains are described in sections XI and XII. The day is grey and the breeze moans, while a wolf pack stalks the horse and its rider, adding a sense of threat. Nature as encountered on this ride is as untamed, wild, and furious as the horse and Mazeppa. Byron emphasizes the seeming boundlessness of nature to create a sense of unreality, giving an almost hallucinatory quality that corresponds to Mazeppa's state of semiconsciousness. Byron seems to want his readers to understand that the quality of the experience is "out of this world," beyond the usual, while he deals at the same time with the most realistic details. One is reminded of Coleridge saying that in working on the *Lyrical Ballads* Wordsworth was supposed to be trying to make the natural seem supernatural. Byron seems to be attempting this same kind of evocation. The landscape is more than descriptive; it is supposed to reinforce the action. This same landscape is rehandled by Hugo in his "Mazeppa" and made ominously significant in the paintings of Vernet and Boulanger.[21]

Beginning in section XIII and ending in the middle of section XVIII, the horse and Mazeppa, the landscape, the ride, and Mazeppa's experience cohere symbolically. Once the horse dies, however, Mazeppa's experience is extended in a new direction, so that all alone he finally comes to grips with life. These central sections are a profound rendering of death and dying and of man's almost unconscious reassertion of life.

Section XIII begins in contradiction: it was an afternoon in June but the air was cold, or it might be that Mazeppa's blood ran cold. The opening may be viewed differently, for fifty years later at this same time of year he will be preparing for the Battle of Poltava.

> Prolong'd endurance tames the bold;
> And I was then not what I seem,
> But headlong as a wintry stream,
> And wore my feelings out before
> I well could count their causes o'er.

>   (XIII, 524–29)

His prolonged suffering calmed his wrath and deadened his senses; he seemed to be wearing out. But, Mazeppa comments, it is no wonder that all this physical torture made him falter for a moment: he is sprung from a race whose passions, when stirred, and when made to suffer, spring and strike when it seems most unlikely, when they seem to be faltering. Mazeppa may or may not realize, for he does not comment about it, that this is what happens to him at the end of the experience; life takes hold of him when he feels death begin to draw him away. A series of similes follow that describe what it is like to be dying, or to be losing consciousness, but Mazeppa, in an aside, admits:

> I own that I should deem it much,
> Dying, to feel the same again;

[21] As Robert F. Gleckner (*Byron and the Ruins of Paradise* [Baltimore: Johns Hopkins Press, 1967], pp. 309–10) says, the landscape is strikingly like that in *The Siege of Corinth*.

> And yet I do suppose we must
> Feel far more ere we turn to dust.
>
>   (XIII, 563–66)

Almost dying is not dying, but

> No matter; I have bared my brow
> Full in Death's face—before—and now.
>
>   (XIII, 567–68)

"Now" is the important word, because Charles XII and his followers are facing death at the hands of the enemy, who surround the camp, if they are caught. Mazeppa, then, has another motive for telling this tale; aside from putting the King to sleep, he wants to bolster the courage of the men in the camp. In section XX, where Mazeppa draws an obvious "moral" from the story, this motive is made explicit.

> What mortal his own doom may guess?
> Let none despond, let none despair!
>
>   (XX, 853–54)

Section XII ends by his drawing together the past and the present in his analysis of almost dying, then breaking his logic and impulsively but sternly asserting his courage—all this to give the men around him heart in what appears to be an inescapably bad situation.

Section XIV introduces a new surge of energy into Mazeppa's story. The rider wavers between consciousness and unconsciousness; he is numb and giddy, but life reasserts its lingering hold. Mazeppa's senses begin to function again and he realizes that he and the horse are in a broad river. The effect: "The waters broke my hollow trance,/ And with a temporary strength/ My stiffen'd limbs were rebaptized." Byron did not see the full symbolic importance of using the word "rebaptized," for here it seems to mean that the water temporarily refreshed rider and horse, or perhaps that Mazeppa has been "rebaptized" into consciousness. No archetypal ritual or spiritual renewal is implied, for the worst of the ordeal is yet to come. The point of the immersion seems to be that Mazeppa should be conscious enough to observe the strange landscape in section XV. The "boundless plain" is before them and "seems,/ Like precipices in our dreams,/ To stretch beyond the sight. . . ." The utter loneliness of this landscape could not be dispelled by illusions, for even

the magic-like phenomena of nature did not deceive him into believing
that any human being was about.

Section XVI begins with a description of the horse slackening his
pace—"His savage force at length o'erspent." But the horse's new tame-
ness was of no use to Mazeppa, who was still so bound to the animal
that all attempts to free himself only continued to produce pain. Dawn
comes with all its misleading associations: "The dizzy race seem'd almost
done,/ Although no goal was nearly won:/ Some streaks announced the
coming sun. . . ." The slowness of its coming seems linked to the abat-
ing of the horse's swiftness and not to some optimistic indication that the
ordeal is nearly over. Only in a general way might the dawn suggest
Mazeppa's ultimate success at the end of the ordeal. The dawn is beautiful but the impression of the place—solitary and silent—is what stays in
the reader's mind. Of course, thus far all these signs of nature are seen
from Mazeppa's point of view. The final throes of his ordeal begin, however, with the horse's death.

The horse seems oblivious to all nature—the river, the plains, the
forests—as he races relentlessly toward some goal. The slowness of the
coming of the dawn in this special place is an indication that he is arriv-
ing close to his goal; the horse staggers to his homeland.

Suddenly in the silence appear a thousand wild horses. Byron con-
trasts the freedom of the herd with the bondage of the horse upon whose
back Mazeppa is bound. The implication of the horse's return is that he
came all this way to die within sight of this herd as well as in this place.
When the horse sees the others, "The sight renerved my courser's feet,/
. . . with a faint low neigh, / He answer'd, and then fell." Is the horse's
return like the return of the exile, the emigré, or the runaway? Each finally returns home to die happily or else dreams about it. Byron himself
was an exile in a land of exiles when he wrote *Mazeppa*. That sense of
nostalgia for one's country and the nationalistic fervor sometimes associated with it were characteristic of the Romantics. Byron is daring to
suggest these feelings for a country through the horse's return to its
homeland. Or, the horde of wild horses may have reminded him of the
wild Cossack bands that roamed the steppes, or even of those wild horse-
men he saw when he visited Ali Pasha. These horses suggest more to
the reader than just the insertion of an interesting episode. Byron chose
to describe ". . . one black mighty steed/ Who seem'd the patriarch of

his breed," which reminds one of the role that Mazeppa will play among the Cossacks as their leader.[22] What Mazeppa saw that day suggests what would happen to him. It is almost as though his horse were trying to demonstrate, to point through his own life and death, what Mazeppa could expect. Mazeppa's horse falls and dies, leaving "the dying on the dead!" Mazeppa has been delivered to his new homeland where he will undergo a last trial alone before being saved, the prelude to his role as Hetman of the Ukraine.

Mazeppa's lonely ordeal begins in the last part of section XVII. The horse's death leads Mazeppa to believe that he will die, too. He begins to feel that his death at this time and place is inevitable, even a boon. His reaction to death is the ambiguous one of most men:

> At times both wish'd for and implored,
> At times sought with self-pointed sword,
> Yet still a dark and hideous close
> To even intolerable woes,
> And welcome in no shape.
>
> (XVII, 731–35)

This section lengthens into a meditation upon death, and Mazeppa's comments apply to the current events as well as to his general philosophical position. His argument runs: the sons of pleasure seem to die "calmer oft than he/ Whose heritage was misery." The implication of Mazeppa's observation is that Charles's death may be more difficult than his own. The man who has tasted *all* that is beautiful and new has no regrets and no hopes, yet the prospect of tomorrow contains potential novelty; tomorrow one may repay and repair, too. The thought of the future makes men want to live and not die. This "moral" is repeated explicitly in section XX. As a result, there is still hope that Charles and his group will escape, that Poltava will be rewon, that Charles will reconquer his now lost lands; tomorrow holds all these possibilities. The reader knows, however, that tomorrow does not hold such promise for Mazeppa.

Section XVIII returns to the "dying on the dead," to Mazeppa chained to the "chill and stiffening steed," to the sinking sun, to his

[22] It may be that Byron was also influenced by Shelley's "black Tartarian horse of giant frame" in Canto VI of *Revolt of Islam*, which was published in 1818, just a year before *Mazeppa*.

moment of hopelessness. Images of death prevail. Mazeppa sees a raven hovering over him, waiting for him to die. The bird comes closer and closer as Mazeppa seems to get nearer to death. The bird was so close at one point that Mazeppa could have touched him, but he lacked the strength. Mazeppa thinks he is near the point of death. A "slight motion of my hand,/ And feeble scratching of the hand,/ The excited throat's struggling noise"—these gestures frightened the bird and death away. Mazeppa breaks his story with "I know no more." His reason did not comprehend what happened next, but he went on to "know" from the dream he had. He recalls a star he fixed his gaze upon, and its pulsing light was like the pulsing of life in him—the "Sensation of recurring sense,/ And then subsiding back to death." He registered his last impressions before subsiding into unconsciousness.

The next section begins "I wake." Whereas this ordeal began with the leaving of "the last of human sounds," it ends with his seeing first a human face, that of a lovely girl, a Cossack maid, who recalls Theresa because of whose love he was forced to undergo this entire ordeal. Section XIX explains how Mazeppa came back to life among the Cossacks. The poem ends somewhat abruptly. Mazeppa draws the obvious "moral" mentioned before:

> Thus the vain fool who strove to glut
> His rage, refining on my pain,
> Sent forth to the wilderness,
> Bound, naked, bleeding, and alone,
> To pass the desert to a throne,—
> What mortal his own doom may guess?
> Let none despond, let none despair!
>
> (XX, 848–854)

He adds that tomorrow there is hope; they may cross the Dnieper and be at ease upon Turkish soil. He goes to bed immediately.

The reader is left with the strange information in the final lines that Charles has been asleep for an hour. These lines are less ironic than they are consistent with the general idea of the poem that man, being so preoccupied with himself, does not listen to others and therefore does not learn his lesson; he falls asleep in the middle of it. The ending can also be explained from the situation in the poem itself. Charles has asked Mazeppa to tell the story so that he might fall asleep, and Mazeppa has complied. From the information about Charles's moral strength in the poem, one understands that his own morale does not have to be bolstered, but his men's does. Although the men do not comment—in fact they hardly seem present at all—Mazeppa is directing his story to them while he is entertaining and instructing the King. Unfortunately, no one really listens.

The focus of the whole poem has been on this death-in-life experience and has led a number of critics to give it a metaphysical interpretation. Englaender was the first to point out that Mazeppa's youthful experiences are stories of crime and punishment, and that the Hetman is a representative of the silent suffering hero possessing great endurance. Englaender draws some of his parallels between images and ideas in *Mazeppa* and the "Rime of the Ancient Mariner" and "The Prisoner of Chillon." [23] Even after close reading, one feels that Mazeppa's experience of death-in-life simply does not have the metaphysical implications Englaender suggests. His interpretation gave William Marshall a foundation for a deeper reading of *Mazeppa* in which he finds archetypal patterns.

The story as it is told by Mazeppa becomes, therefore, one of ordeal and survival in which the survivors seem to have to elect. The solitary nature of the experience is essential. The tale is not unlike the stories of fall and redemption, of death and rebirth, except that in the words of the garrulous and egoistic old man it becomes an unconscious travesty of these. There is sin but not atonement, rescue but no salvation, recollection but no selfless understanding. [24]

That is to say, Mazeppa does commit a crime, but he is not really punished for it. Graham Hough goes a step further to explain that paradox:

What was meant as a punishment brought him [Mazeppa] a throne. I need hardly labor to explain the symbolism; Mazeppa has sinned through passion; he is given a punishment that fits the crime—delivered over to a force more wild and tameless than himself; his own will and power of control is completely suspended. His wild horse carries him to the land of wild horses—the realm that is to say where the untamed passions are at home. This looks like the end of his earthly career, but he survives the ordeal and emerges renewed and powerful, a king among his own people. [25]

[23] Englaender, pp. 9ff.

[24] William H. Marshall, *The Structure of Byron's Major Poems* (Philadelphia: University of Pennsylvania Press, 1962), p. 123.

[25] Graham Hough, *Image and Experience* (Lincoln: University of Nebraska Press, 1960), p. 139.

Mazeppa is essentially a symbolic poem, but the readings of it by Englaender, Marshall, and Hough, though perhaps valid in spirit, somehow miss the elemental symbolism at the cost of a more complex interpretation that the poem itself does not support. One should ask oneself whether or not Byron is really trying to overturn the general moral view that crime must be punished. The poem is in no sense saying obliquely that in some cases, Mazeppa's in particular, crime is rewarded. It only incidentally uses the crime-and-punishment motif, which it relates only to Byron's treatment of Mazeppa as a mild version of the Noble Outlaw. Mazeppa is mainly an urbane courtier whose passions are untamed and who pays what seems an exaggerated price for his crime. As far as Mazeppa is concerned, all's for love, and that is still his motto at seventy.

Byron is not interested in metaphysics in the poem, and the symbolism operates on a simpler level. First, in the death-in-life experience the horse, ride, and landscape fuse in Mazeppa to give a symbolic rendering of his state of being, which fluctuates from anger, frustration, and brute physical strength to exhaustion, passivity, and death. Man and animal drained of all their energies is conveyed in a nondescriptive nonexpository way. Metaphor, simile, analogy are used on many levels, and juxtaposition is employed to try to create a symbolic fusion. Byron attempts, with less success, to do something similar with a death-in-life experience in "The Prisoner of Chillon." The Prisoner's "I know not why/ I could not die,/ I had no earthly hope—but faith,/ And that forbade a selfish death" is close to Mazeppa's state of being in section XVII, 740ff. Of course Bonnivard and Mazeppa are very different types, but Byron deals cursorily with their characters in both cases to get at each man's experience of almost dying. The Prisoner's trance is so described:

> What next befell me then and there
> I know not well—I never knew;
> First came the loss of light, and air,
> And then the darkness too.
> I had no thought, no feeling—none—
> Among the stones I stood a stone.
>
> (IX, 231–36)

Here in brief, almost expository terms is something akin to Mazeppa's moving into unconsciousness in section XVIII. Both are brought to life by a bird: the Prisoner's is a beautiful song bird, Mazeppa's a raven; the

former is a sign of life, the latter of death. In "The Prisoner of Chillon,"
however, Byron does not render these feelings; he seems content there to
explain them.

Byron also uses some of these same images in "Ode on Venice," published with *Mazeppa* in 1819; this time he transfers the experience of
dying from men into personifications such as Hope, Faintness, and
Death itself, which in turn relate to the death of liberty in Venice.

> But there are better than the gloomy errors,
> The weeds of nations in their last decay,
> When Vice walks forth with her unsoften'd terrors,
> And Mirth is madness, and but smiles to slay;
> And Hope is nothing but a false delay,
> The sick man's lightning half an hour ere death,
> When Faintness, the last mortal birth of Pain,
> And apathy of limb, the dull beginning
> Of the cold staggering race which Death is winning,
> Steals vein by vein and pulse by pulse away;
> Yet so relieving the o'er-tortured clay,
> To him appears renewal of his breath,
> And freedom the mere numbness of his chain;—
> And then he talks of life, and how again
> He feels his spirits soaring—albeit weak,
> And of the fresher air, which he would seek;
> And as he whispers knows not that he gasps,
> That his thin finger feels not what it clasps,
> And so the film comes o'er him—and the dizzy
> Chamber swims round and round—and shadows busy,
> At which he vainly catches, flit and gleam,
> Till the last rattle chokes the strangled scream,
> And all is ice and blackness,—and the earth
> That which it was the moment ere our birth.
>
> (32–55)

The images are built on death or that time a "half hour ere death"; the
central action in *Mazeppa* takes place during that same state. "Hope"
becomes the sick man and a long metaphor develops through lines 37–55.
Lines 38–41 characterize the state of semiconsciousness, of pain, and of
impending death. The "cold staggering race which Death is winning"
reminds one of Mazeppa's whole ride, Death having won the horse's life
and nearly Mazeppa's. Lines 42–43 explain how faintness gives the illusion of renewal, and one recalls Mazeppa's "temporary strength" and
how inevitable death seemed a boon to him at that time. From line 44 to

the end of the section Byron is describing those same feelings of dying that one grasps in much greater detail and depth in *Mazeppa*, but in the "Ode" he emphasizes the illusion of hope.

The great difference among the poems is the way in which the same imagery is handled. In the "Prisoner of Chillon" and "Ode on Venice" Byron merely describes the experience of almost dying, yet even in them one feels that the whole experience has more significance for him, a significance which he tries to convey more clearly in each reworking of the same basic materials. The three poems deal with some form of imprisonment that leads its victim through physical suffering (in a metaphorical sense when he writes of Venice) almost to the point of death, and all are associated with the suppression of personal and political liberty. A bird in a cage, a man in prison, a soul imprisoned in a body of clay, a man tied to a horse seem to be among his favorite images at this time, but only in *Mazeppa* does the imagery form a symbolic construct in the reader's mind. Mazeppa's ride and the horse's fury, flight, and death render the feelings of a patriot dedicated to the liberty of men—liberty understood in its widest sense. Such is the meaning of the central episode of *Mazeppa*, but the wild ride is not the whole poem.

Byron, ultimately a realist and on the alert for the irony of fate, sets the symbol in a historical frame, which, as pointed out, is defeat. Mazeppa loses the Battle of Poltava, his hetmanate, and soon after, his life. Byron will not alter these facts and thereby falsify his hero. He seems to have loved Mazeppa's daring and endurance, his wit and humor, and the achievement of his life; but he could not overlook the man's flaws and ultimate downfall. If Byron liked to raise men to the level of gods, to admire figures who seemed apart from the herd of men, and to try to explore the landscape of their souls in his poems, he also realized that such were most often brought low by fate, that they suffered the passions and guilt of common men, and that their inner lives were an enigma to themselves and to those around them. Byron never quite believed in the heroes and symbols of his own creation and that doubt crept into his poems—*Mazeppa* in this case. Critics have felt that *Mazeppa* is a poem "between" poems, perhaps because the satiric strain in Byron was becoming stronger and stronger, but was not intense enough to be the attitude of a serious hero: Don Juan had already overtaken his imagination, and Childe Harold was slipping away.

Critical considerations of *Mazeppa*, however, that focus on its uneven tone or that find its hero an inadequate Byronic creation miss the poet's experiments with symbolism. Byron's attempts to render the death-in-life experience and to demonstrate how it bears upon personal and political freedom should make readers wary of assuming that Byron is only a discursive poet. *Mazeppa* is much less a failure of combining two disparate styles of poetry and much more an effort to write in a new style. Ultimately, Byron was more comfortable with irony, but before that attitude came to dominate his poetry, he ventured into symbolism. The subsequent influence of the poem dealt with either the symbolic ride, as in Hugo's lyric and the paintings of the French Romantics, or it utilized the themes of history and freedom, as in the poetry of Ryleev, Pushkin, and the Slavic circle. Byron's continental readers were more appreciative of *Mazeppa* and had greater insight into the form and content of the poem than was the English audience.[26]

[26] In 1820 the only "artistic" response in England was *Mazeppa Travestied: a Poem*, with an introductory address to the goddess of "Milling," and her worshipper, "The Fancy."

3.

MAZEPPA AMONG
THE FRENCH ROMANTICS

*It is not Mazeppa you carry there, I say,
but a corpse! You are not going to a throne
but toward a tomb!*

BY 1839, PETRUS BOREL's readers knew enough about Mazeppa to catch
the allusion, but by 1839 French Romanticism had taken a new turn.
The generation of 1830, to subdue its boredom, had turned to the grotesque,[1] so that one no longer wrote about a suffering Mazeppa but
about a sinister one: the heroes of the 1820s became grim, possessed
creatures in the 1830s. The battle of *Hernani* had been won and the grey
cloud of a new revolution hung over Europe. Victor Hugo, one of the
first spokesmen for the French Romantics, wrote to his friend Louis
Boulanger, the painter, from Vevey in 1837:

Night—it was yesterday—I walked along the shore of the lake and thought about
you a lot, Louis, and of our pleasant walks in 1828, when we were twenty-four,
when you were doing *Mazeppa*, when I was doing *Les Orientales*, when we were
contented by a horizontal ray of sunlight on the sleeping waters on Vaugirard.[2]

Those days, those works, those subjects had passed, lamentably gone
by. The 1820s were great and exciting times for French Romanticism,
for Hugo became the Cyclops, as Ste.-Beuve called him, of French literature with his *Odes et Ballades*, *Les Orientales*, and *Cromwell*; Lamartine

---

[1] Edmond Estève, *Byron et le romantisme française* (Paris, 1907), p. 226.
[2] Victor Hugo *Oeuvres complètes de Victor Hugo* 45 vols. (Paris, 1904–1913), Poésie 1:783,
quoting an article of René Doumic, "Les derniers travaux sur Leconte de Lisle," *Revue des
Deux Mondes* (15 juillet 1909).

published his *Méditations poétiques,* a literary sensation; Stendhal published *De l'amour* and *Racine et Shakespeare;* Géricault and Delacroix infused French painting with new dynamism; and Louis Boulanger startled the viewers of the Salon of 1827 with his painting *The Agony of Mazeppa.* It was foremost the decade when French Romanticism began to define itself, and Mazeppa was part of it.

The interest in Mazeppa must first of all be attributed to the ever-increasing popularity of Byron's poetry in France beginning about 1815 and to the vogue for *byronisme,* that cult for the man in his poetry and the poetry in the man that swept from Paris to Moscow in the first half of the nineteenth century. Edmond Estève, relying upon Charles Nodier's interpretation of Byron in 1823,[3] explains that by 1815 "the germs of future byronisme had begun to appear in European literature: they were, however, suspended and floating. France, represented by Rousseau, Voltaire, and Chateaubriand, had furnished a good part. England and Germany, Young, Goethe, Schiller gave the rest. These crossing elements met in the soul of a great poet and were amalgamated there." [4]

Of course, it was out of general Anglomania that enthusiasm began to grow for Byron. Ste.-Beuve's interest in "les Lakistes," the rediscovery of Shakespeare and the famous performances of *Hamlet* and *Othello* that aroused such controversy because they were performed in English by the Penley Troupe in 1822 (but were a theatrical triumph in 1828) and the passion of Sir Walter Scott's novels (translated into French almost as soon as they came off English presses) all formed an important English backdrop for the French Romantics of the 1820s. Byron, however, stands out conspicuously.

The most significant event in the progress of Byron's popularity in France took place in 1818, when the Galignani brothers began to publish an English edition of his complete works in Paris, and a year later the complete works in French began to appear, translated by Amadée Pichot and Eusèbe de Salle. *Mazeppa,* first published in London in 1819, was simultaneously published by the Galignani house in Paris, though it was called the second edition.[5] *Mazeppa* was the first addition to the complete works in English, and subsequently a translation was included in the Pichot-de Salle edition.

[3] Charles Nodier, *Annales,* 12 (1823): 196–97.   [4] Estève, p. 20.
[5] Also appearing in 1819 was an edition in Boston.

Byron's Oriental Tales were considered by Europeans as a new literary genre, using a new subject matter. It is no coincidence that Victor Hugo called his 1829 collection of poems *Les Orientales*, for he wanted his readers to remember, among other associations, Byron's poems, if only to understand how he, using some of Byron's subject matter, extended it in new directions. When *Mazeppa* was first published in Paris it was billed as an Oriental Tale, but at the time the reading public's Byronic passion was for *Manfred*, which not only gives a clear picture of the Byronic hero but also of *byronisme*. The term suggested a highly individualistic character with lyrical and aristocratic overtones. Such a character was in revolt against society and life itself; he was restless and obsessed with the problem of destiny.[6] The French, who already had hints of these traits in Rousseau and Chateaubriand, saw them fuse dramatically in one man and his work. The malaise of the French artist after the defeat of Napoleon and the frustrating sameness in art before the Romantic *échec* were reinforced by Byron's malaise, by his Harold and Manfred.

The first review of Byron's *Mazeppa* to appear in France was written by the young Alfred de Vigny in 1820. It is worth quoting from at length to see how little is said about the poem itself and how much, on the other hand, is implied about Byron.

Mazeppa is an extraordinary effort of a very rich imagination, for who but Lord Byron would dare to compose a poem from the simple speech of a man carried on a savage horse? Who else could succeed? Consider a work in which, with the faithful and elegant painting of places and scenes, in which the author joined that with the shock of passion rendered by the expression of flame; a work in which appears a character always so tired of life and tormented by profound despair that the feeling of a secret but deserved pain or a criminal remorse is impressed in his heart, and you would have an idea of the composition of Lord Byron— perhaps then you would also understand his character.[7]

The French artists who treat Mazeppa seem almost to pick up de Vigny's challenge and try to fuse landscape, passion, torment, and despair into their creations. De Vigny describes here the characteristics of Romantic ennui, which Byron seems to have projected from his own life into the lives of his characters. To be sure, de Vigny's interpretation is a

[6] Estève, pp. 23, 28, 32.
[7] Alfred de Vigny, *Conservateur Littéraire* 3 (December, 1820): 212–16.

special reading of the work, and it is difficult to find in the words of
Byron's poem. What Byron actually said and what the French thought
he said were often different, but it was the latter that interested them.
That Byron and his works were difficult to separate in their imaginations
was a manifestation of a particular interest of the French Romantics, who
were fascinated by the artist himself and what his work of art said about
him. De Vigny is not being casual when he begins by calling the reader's
attention to "an extraordinary effort of a very rich imagination," which is
really a definition of a work of art. The act of artistic creation is the subject of many French Romantic works, and so it is that Mazeppa becomes
a useful subject for them. Whereas they interpreted Byron's *Mazeppa* as a
paradigm of the poet's life—Byron's or any artist's—they saw Mazeppa
as a paradigm for the artist himself. Byron seemed hardly preoccupied
with himself as an artist, and his Oriental Tales and his dramas were
more studies of various personalities and characters in action. The
French, interested as they were in subjective analyses, often read
Byron's works as though they were autobiographical. They seem to have
assumed that everything Byron wrote was to be read as *Childe Harold*.
French artists most often seemed to have a sense that they were different
from other men for "artistic" reasons. For them, the Romantic period
was in part an intense exploration of what an artist was, not through the
philosophical speculation of, for instance, Coleridge and Shelley, but
through actual works of art.

The French Romantic artist, then, looked upon Byron and his creations as projections of the artist; Mazeppa became in their minds less a
historical figure and more an expression of Byron, and even more, a
model of the artist. But Mazeppa was not only written about in France,
he was also painted by some of the greatest artists: Géricault, Delacroix,
and Horace Vernet. And there is a relation, sometimes explicit, between
the paintings and the poems.

Many French Romantic painters were not interested in merely illustrating a poem but wanted to capture the "poetry" on canvas. They often
searched for the right scene in a poem, a scene that would convey the
whole work. In one way it is not difficult to understand why the Romantics would be interested in transforming poetry into painting, since the
inspiration could have come from the poetry itself, which was highly
descriptive and "scenic." Byron, for instance, turned Childe Harold's

grand tour into a spiritual journey, often describing the natural and man-made world with the eye of an archeologist. One often sees in his poetry a desire to make the described natural world a background that illumi-nates feelings and ideas. There was a growing sense that merely describ-ing was not enough, as *Mazeppa* already illustrated; nature had to relate to or suggest other things. French Romantic poetry, though often merely highly descriptive, as for instance Lamartine's *Méditations*, acquired more symbolic overtones. Many of de Vigny's poems move into symbolism, although it is fairly conventional, and one sees the clear symbolic devel-opment in Hugo's poetry as it matures. A poem as early as "Mazeppa" is already half symbol. The impact of the theory of the relation of painting to poetry can be seen in the very vocabulary of French Romantic poets, which is filled with terms taken from painting. The metaphor for poet is frequently painter; he paints with words. In his review of *Mazeppa*, de Vigny talks about the "faithful and elegant painting of places and scenes," an idea that permeated not only his artistic sensibility but also that of many of his contemporaries.

Painting and poetry are perhaps more closely related in French Ro-manticism than, for instance, in German or English, where one does have the examples of Blake and Keats, because of a special set of circum-stances and people. French Romantics had to fight a battle of aesthetics (sometimes it became physical) against their neoclassical predecessors. Géricault's *Raft of the Medusa* caused a scandal and furor in the Salon of 1819, and proved to be the warning shot for what was to come. The painting was a sudden departure in subject and style from the prevailing though effete neoclassical standard. The years 1820–24 saw the creations of more artistic departures: *Dante's Barque*, *The Massacre at Scio*, and the statue of the *Grand Condée*, to mention the most important. By the end of 1824 the old guard had become generally ineffectual; Louis David was in exile, Girodet was dead, Gérard had defected, Gros was weak; as a result the new art gradually took hold. In retrospect, one can see that the 1820s saw a radical shift in artistic sensibility—a conscious revolution in taste—among the young, talented artists in France.

The shift in painting and sculpture was at approximately the same time reflected in literature. French Romantic painters, critics, poets, and novelists, in the tradition of the salon, often gathered together for social-intellectual exchanges in Toulouse, Rouen, and of course Paris. One such center of artistic activity was Victor Hugo's house, where of an evening in the 1820s one might have found Louis Boulanger, Ste.-Beuve, Théophile Gautier, Gérard de Nerval, Vinces, Parnie, Ernest de Saxe-Cobourg, Achille and Eugène Devéria, Céléstin Nanteuil, Edouard Thiery, Petrus Borel and his two brothers, Achille Roche, de Vigny, Delacroix, de Musset, the Jahonnots, Dumas, Brizeux, Edouard Fouinet, Fonteny, and others.

Ideas, subjects, theories, and techniques were undoubtedly discussed and interchanged, and an incalculable and unrecordable kind of mutual influence took place. Such salons or *cénacles* were the classrooms where the French Romantic school created and defined itself. In the 1820s Hugo gave special attention to the painters at the *cénacle*, for he himself painted, as did de Musset, Théophile Gautier, and Auguste de Châtillon. He was also encouraging his close friend Louis Boulanger and exhibiting his works to the group. Some of the artists illustrated the poems and novels of their *cénacle* companions and did the sets and decor for their plays at the Comédie Française. Hugo's salon was, all in all, a milieu conducive to art and ideas where painters and writers alike might come upon a subject to their liking, discuss it, and decide to use it, each in his own medium. Byron moved Delacroix and Géricault as much as he did Hugo. Delacroix responded to Shakespeare the same way Hugo and Ste.-Beuve did. In such a milieu the French Romantics could support one another and encourage each other in what they clearly understood was a revolution of artistic sensibility. To be sure, they disagreed and they formed no league or conspiracy to overthrow the old guard of academicians and neoclassicists—as Gautier pointed out in his *Histoire de Romantisme*—but they seem to have had a good deal of mutual respect for each other's work and a wide understanding of what they wanted to see eliminated from art. And in a few cases—Mazeppa's in particular—there was a direct influence upon a work by artists working in other media. These special circumstances of French art in the 1820s helped immensely to bring painting close to literature at the inception of the Romantic school in France.

The French Romantic painters were particularly interested in horses—a theme, one may recall, that seems to have roots deep in the European consciousness. According to Léon Rosenthal, the French painters' passion for the horse took hold in the atelier of the famous painter and

teacher Carles Vernet; [8] however, the subject had been used extensively in England in the eighteenth century by Stubbs, Fuseli, and Ward. Gros, Auguste, Géricault, Delacroix, Boulanger, and Vernet knew much of that English painting and may have introduced the theme into their work as a result of this influence. Many times the horse is associated with Arab themes and generally eastern themes in France; this association recalls Byron's Oriental Tales, which inspired a number of them. Horses were, of course, as ordinary as trees in the early nineteenth century, for they were used for all kinds of work and recreation, as well as for transportation. In looking through Géricault's work, for instance, one sees hundreds of pictures of ordinary horses in everyday settings. But in certain others, the painter's attention focused upon the animal's beauty, its powerful muscles, and the tension in its body. It begins to suggest passion and spirit, conveying a powerfully noble suffering to the viewer. There is a sense that in its struggle to free itself the horse is revolting against all that binds it—harness, reins, saddle, and man. For the French, such a horse became an analogue for the artist who felt the same way, and in French Romantic paintings Mazeppa is added to the theme of the horse.

Werner Hofmann's remarks about Mazeppa in Romantic painting apply as well to horses and to their appearance in literature: "Mazeppa is not only the man who is defeated by the dark powers of animalism, but he is also the outlaw and rightless man whom society rejects and mercilessly delivers over to ruin. He is, to quote a catchword, 'man in revolt.' " [9] The French Romantic artist saw himself in revolt against a society that produced a lonely and terrifying suffering and anguish: his whole story was analogous to the suffering of Mazeppa during his ride. A cruel and insensitive society had rejected Mazeppa and had imposed a stringent punishment that he endured at great physical and mental expense, but ultimately he would triumph to become Hetman. So the French artist saw his punishment, pain, and ultimate triumph as characteristic of the unrecognized genius.

As pointed out earlier, Byron's *Mazeppa* did not catch the French

[8] Léon Rosenthal, *La peinture romantique: essai sur l'évolution de la peinture française de 1815 à 1830* (Paris, n.d.), p. 133.

[9] Werner Hofmann, *The Earthly Paradise: Art in the Nineteenth Century* (New York: G. Braziller, 1961), p. 240.

imagination as soon as it was published in Paris. In 1820, the year of de Vigny's review of *Mazeppa*, Théodore Géricault left for England to tour with the *Raft of the Medusa*. He had been a student of Carles Vernet, Horace's father, for about two years and later of Pierre Guérin, with whom he learned the theory and practice of neoclassical art under the influence of Louis David. But by 1820 he had worked out his own unique and startling style. All along he had been painting and sketching horses; they now began to take on a heavy sensual quality with mystical overtones, not unlike what D. H. Lawrence would do with a horse in prose a hundred years later. Marcel Brion points out that Géricault's love for horses surpasses any other artist's. He knew almost as much about them as Franconi, the famous equestrian star at the Cirque Olympique.[10] He went to England to make money but while there he became fascinated with lithography and the life and works of Lord Byron. Perhaps Géricault was more attracted to the horses in Byron's Oriental Tales than to the heroes and their ennui. In 1819–20, he published two lithographs, *Lara Wounded* and *The Giaour*, where the subjects are really the horses and not the men.[11]

Géricault returned from England at the end of 1821, and in 1823, he and Eugène Lami published four lithographs: *Mazeppa, The Giaour, Lara,* and the *Bride of Abydos*.[12] The lithograph of Mazeppa, according to Charles Clément, illustrates the lines from Byron's *Mazeppa* in section XVII: "Le coursier tente de s'élever sur le rivage, qui semble le repousser; ses poils et sa crinière sont luisants et humides"; however, this rather loose translation actually comes from section XV, 601–4: "With glossy skin, and dripping mane,/ And reeling limbs, and reeking flesh,/ The wild steed'd sinewy nerves still strain/ Up the repelling bank." The center of the picture, as either quotation leads one to believe, is the horse. Mazeppa is tied so that his body is stretched across the horse's back, his head tilted back over the horse's right haunch. One is struck by the contrast between Mazeppa's naked body and the horse's. The horse

---

[10] Marcel Brion, *Romantic Art* (New York: McGraw-Hill, 1960), p. 134.

[11] Estève, p. 193.

[12] Reproduced in black and white in Dénise Aimé-Azam, *Mazeppa, Géricault et son temps* (Paris, 1954); see also Charles Clément, *Géricault: étude biographique et critique avec le catalogue raisonnée de l'oeuvre du maître* (Paris, 1868), p. 406; *Géricault dans les collections privées français,* Exposition organisée au bénéfice de la societé des amis du Louvre, 6 novembre–7 decembre 1964, entry 32.

is a brown bay; his body is turned to the left and he is trying to get a
hold on the river bank to lift himself and his burden out of the water. It
is a dramatic picture, showing the animal at a moment of uncertainty,
expending tremendous energy. The horse's straining is clearly in contrast to Mazeppa's helplessness, and the general impression created by
both man and horse is an exquisite tension. The pain and torture in the
drawing are subsumed by the beauty of both bodies—a pictorial embodiment of the "Romantic agony." [13]

Clément lists in his catalogue another Mazeppa drawing done between
1820 and 1824, perhaps a study for this published one, in which the emphasis shifts to Mazeppa. The horse is dead and has his back to the
viewer.[14] Mazeppa, nude and dying, has his left leg caught under the
horse's body, his torso thrust forward, with his head tossed back, his
legs and thighs thrust to the forefront. Again, his body is twisted and
taut in such a way that the impression is one of tension. Géricault may
have had in mind Byron's line "the dying on the dead" when doing this
drawing. Here more than in the first one feels the sensual beauty of pain.
Aimé-Azam, who owns the original of the first lithograph and has written a popular biography of Géricault that focuses eccentrically upon this
painting, interprets it as a symbol of the painter himself:

Géricault himself would not point it out: this horse is the form of his destiny, the
path to his death. Its royalty, however! . . . Never again did Géricault cry for
those impossible loves, for his union with torment, his subjection to the gallop of
the wild horse, which was his life, as in his blue Mazeppa.[15]

Whether or not the work does all of that is doubtful, but it does capture the anguish of a mind that seems to be "half in love with easeful
death," and Byron's Mazeppa had undergone its first transformation into
a new art form. From a few lines that struck his imagination, Géricault
produced two pictures showing bodies, man and animal, strained to their
breaking point, but beautifully so. They suggest a pair that is almost
erotic, a tension that is about to break into tears and blood. The torture
could be an embodiment of Géricault's feelings, but be that as it may,
Mazeppa's legend had found a new interpreter.

[13] According to Clément, this lithograph, the best of the four, had been completely re-
touched by Géricault in pencil.

[14] Clément, p. 365.   [15] Aimé-Azam, p. 260.

Géricault died early in January 1824, and on the 27th, Eugene Delacroix heard of his death. They had many things in common, especially
their love of literature and horses, but there was a difference in degree.
Delacroix loved literature more and horses less. He had a penchant for
the theater and the novel of action that inspired many of his paintings:
scenes from *Faust*, *Goetz von Berlichingen*, *Hamlet*, the *Corsair*, *Lara*, the
Giaour, and *Ivanhoe*. He admired greatly the work of Berlioz, who was
trying to capture the essence of literary works in much of his program
music. He was a great admirer of Byron's work, which he could read
well in English. Delacroix would in fact use subjects from Byron until
1855, when he did the *Two Foscari*. Berlioz and Delacroix seemed to
respond to literature in the same way and their expression is often similar, though it takes the form of music in one and painting in the other.
Liszt's piano étude "Mazeppa" and his symphonic poem of the same title
are attempts to capture the anguish and triumph of Mazeppa's ride in
music and are greatly influenced by Berlioz's and Delacroix's transformation of literature into music and painting respectively. For them, most or
all of a work of literature had to be transformed into one visual or aural
experience, and the spirit and meaning had to be realized therein. For
Géricault the literary influence seemed to be less encompassing, more a
focusing on a few lines, on a beautiful moment of power, though he was
able to convey the passionate nature of both man and beast. For Delacroix the literary influence was more grand, broader in its influence: an
attempt to make a statement beyond the expression of passion.

In late April or early May 1824, Delacroix began to buy the small
works of Géricault, the dead painter being much on Delacroix's mind.
"Poor Géricault! I saw you descend into a steady decline where there are
no more dreams." [16] He says impulsively, "How I would like to be a
poet. But at least, to produce paintings. Do that mainly, daringly. What
a choice to make! Do engravings of paintings if painting fails you, and
huge canvases." All this time he is addressing Géricault. His most instructive remark follows: "The poet is very rich; recall, to enflame your-
self eternally, certain passages of Byron; they do me good. The end of
the *Bride of Abydos*, the *Death of Selim*, his body tossed on the waves and
that hand especially, that hand raised by the wave that is going to die on

---

[16] André Joubin, ed., *Journal de Eugène Delacroix* (Paris, 1932), 1:94, 114–16.

the shore. That is sublime and only to him. I sense those things as a painter is allowed to." [17] Here is the literary mode transformed into painting and the painting into literature. It is what Delacroix sensed in Géricault's work and tried himself to create in his own.

In 1824, Delacroix did a *Mazeppa* that contained few changes from Gèricault's lithograph.[18] He was inspired no doubt by his feelings for the dead artist, by his love for Byron's poetry, and by the subject matter. In the same year Delacroix did two sketches of Mazeppa inspired by section IX of Byron's *Mazeppa* (358–74). Whereas Géricault chose to depict Mazeppa at a point in the agony of his wild ride, Delacroix turned his attention to the moment that Mazeppa was being strapped to the horse. The note in his *Journal* refers to the subject as "*the Struggles of Mazeppa* against those who bound him, with the Palatine's chateau in the background." [19] The work shows one man, apparently a Tartar, restraining the horse, which seems filled with fury and rage and ready to break away at any moment. Two other men, with what seems to be all their might, are trying to tie Mazeppa to the wild animal. This portion of the painting is full of movement, violence, and energy, while the background is a serene landscape showing the Palatine's castle. The revolt, tension, torture, fury in the twisting bodies of the men and animal were precisely what fired Delacroix's imagination.

One's eye is drawn to the central episode of the painting, but if one examines the background, one notices that Delacroix has set Mazeppa against a larger background than has Géricault, and that Delacroix has increased the drama of the center by placing it against a placid landscape that hints at the previous action; the castle stands silent.

René Huyghe's remarks fall short of the impact of the painting: "Géricault celebrated mainly human mastery in bringing the animal, whether horse or bull, to a standstill; this theme did not tempt Delacroix; what attracted him was the theme of Mazeppa, in which the life of the instincts irresistibly and without respite carries away with it the human

[17] *Ibid.*, pp. 99–100.

[18] Alfred Robaut, *L'oeuvre complète de Eugène Delacroix, peintures, dessins, gravures, lithographes catalogué et reproduit* (Paris, 1885), p. 74.

[19] *Journal*, 1:100. This work is called *Mazeppa attaché au cheval sauvage* in Robaut, p. 397; there are also listed eight sketches for the painting in Robaut, p. 398, that I was unable to find reproduced anywhere. See also René Huyghe, *Delacroix* (New York: H. N. Abrams, 1963), plate #329. He says a sketch appears in *Athenaeum*, Helsinki, 1828.

will." [20] Delacroix does seem most interested in presenting the tremendous human struggle and the attempt to bind fury to fury in the horse and man, but he places them in a larger context that calls to mind the poem and suggests a larger conception of the entire subject. He sets the action of his painting in a "frame," much as Byron set his symbol, but Delacroix cannot be construed as being ironic. His "frame" is a deliberate serene contrast to violent action that points up the central meaning of his painting. He has captured an ideal moment in Mazeppa's experience but placed it in space—and even time—more effectively than Byron.

Géricault's and Delacroix's treatments of Mazeppa, although excellent, did not reach a wide audience. In 1826, Horace Vernet, the son of Carles Vernet, Géricault's teacher, painted what was probably the most popular picture of Mazeppa in Europe, *Mazeppa among the Wolves*.[21] Actually, there are two slightly different versions.[22] Vernet's paintings of Mazeppa are, first of all, not so inspired by literature as Géricault's and Delacroix's, for although Vernet knows Byron's poem, he uses it more casually. The wolves are in the poem, but Byron makes very little use of them, descriptive or otherwise; they are merely part of the threatening landscape. Vernet focuses on them, perhaps because Byron does not, and in a way fills in pictorially what Byron left between the lines, allowing Vernet's imagination free reign.

In the first version the horse and his burden are speeding through the wilderness. In the background one can see the wolves coming to attack horse and rider. Mazeppa does not see them but the horse seems to sense them. All are set in a wild, almost fantastic landscape. Mazeppa's body is not tense and strained as it is in Géricault's and Delacroix's paintings but seems quite at ease. He appears to be stretched on the horse's back, as if allowing himself to be carried without putting up any struggle. There is a sense of speed and fury in the painting but no rage. The environment is dark and sinister in a Gothic way, as in section XII of Byron's poem, where Mazeppa appears helpless and senseless in the terrible natural world. Vernet's threatening landscape creates a good atmospheric effect,

[20] Huyghe, p. 451.

[21] Zbigniew Raszewski, *Staroświecczyzna i postęp czasu* (Warsaw, 1963), p. 189.

[22] *Mazeppa aux loups*, the first version, is in the Kunsthalle in Bremen. *Mazeppa enchaîné*, the second, is in the Chapelle de l'Hospice in Avignon. A lithograph by W. Clerc was published in London in 1831. A copy made by Molinari appeared in the *Tygodnik Illustrowany*, no. 57 (1869): 52.

but the passive hero on the plunging horse seems to counter the effect.
The supple body draped over the horse's back is like a reclining nude. In
fact, Mazeppa seems almost effeminate. His body is beautiful in a soft
way (in contrast to the powerful body seen in the depictions of Géricault
and Delacroix) so that Mazeppa seems out of place in the painting.

In the second version, Vernet has the wolves attacking the horse from
three sides; here Mazeppa sees them. His face is filled with terror, but
the rest of his body is the same as in the first version. These slight
changes give the painting more drama, but it still does not cohere because the passivity in the central figure is retained. One could argue that
Byron had described Mazeppa as senseless on most of the ride, making it
virtually impossible for him to respond to any threat except by a facial
expression, but such draining of energy comes later in the poem and simply cannot be depicted in the total subject Vernet chose. In a sense, any
moment in a literary work could be transformed into a painting, or more
aptly an inspiration for a painting, but there are "right" moments, Delacroix would argue, moments that when put on canvas give a total insight
into the subject. Unfortunately, Vernet did not choose such a moment.
Perhaps he was aware of his failure in the first version and tried to cor-
rect it in the second, but without success.

Even though Vernet's paintings of Mazeppa were the most popular in
Europe, it was Louis Boulanger's in the Salon of 1827 that created the
immediate éclat in Hugo's circle. The young Boulanger was a close
friend of Hugo's and in almost constant attendance at his salon in the
1820s. Boulanger and Hugo talked about literature and art intimately,
and Hugo looked upon him as a poet as well as a painter; so did the
cénacle chez Hugo. Evidently, Boulanger's mind was sympathetic to
Hugo's. One suspects, however, that Hugo could dominate him because
Boulanger had only a minor genius for painting and poetry, nothing
comparable to Delacroix's. Hugo's insistence upon Boulanger's genius
gives one the impression of excessive pleading, and it cannot be over-
looked that in very important ways it was Hugo's encouragement and
power that made Boulanger's reputation. His *Witches' Sabbath* hung in
Hugo's salon on the rue Notre-Dame des Champs for all to see. That
kind of compliment from Hugo was a guarantee of success.

It has become difficult to assess the artistic worth of Boulanger's painting of Mazeppa because it became in 1827 a symbol of the triumph of

Romanticism in France. The painters and poets who saw it, first in Hugo's salon and later in the Salon exhibit, probably spoke about it as though it did depict the Romantic artist, but Hugo really put his imprimatur on that interpretation by the kind of poem he wrote about Mazeppa and by his dedication of it to Boulanger. The poets were particularly exultant about Boulanger's painting; Hugo and his circle celebrated it as a victory for one of their own with an assault of lyric commentary such as no painting had received before that time.[23]

Marcel Brion calls Boulanger's *Mazeppa* "a powerfully original picture that revealed the dazzling talent of a twenty-one-year-old painter."[24] The *cénacle* in Paris in 1827 may have felt that way about it, but surely the twentieth-century viewer does not. First of all, the work is not so original. Delacroix had already shown "a static phase of the Mazeppa story . . . the moment when the rebel is tied to his horse."[25] Boulanger takes the same central action of Delacroix's painting and expands the background. It seems odd that no one has pointed out the similarity before. Boulanger and Delacroix met one another in Hugo's salon and could have spoken about it; or, most likely, Boulanger saw Delacroix's work and was inspired by it.[26] Boulanger seems to have recapitulated some of the dramatic quality of Delacroix in his depiction of the horse and Mazeppa and to have even given some form to Géricault's energy and anguish, to which he has added voluptuousness of Vernet. He expands Delacroix's background by adding the characters of the Palatine and the judges who he assumed condemned Mazeppa to this punishment.

Boulanger's work does have overtones of hate and animal fury, and it is also more literary than Delacroix's: the story of crime, punishment, judgment, and execution are obvious at a glance. Delacroix, however, had a better sense of balance between action and background. Boulanger simply adds too much "story" to his painting by crowding the canvas

[23] Marie Aristide, *Le peintre poète Louis Boulanger* (Paris, 1925), p. 24.

[24] Brion, p. 142.

[25] *Ibid.*

[26] Boulanger's painting hangs in the Rouen Museum. A lithograph was published by Bès and Dubreuil c. 1830 (reprinted in 1855). It can be seen in the Bibliothèque Nationale (Cabinet des Estampes). See also Aristide, p. 22.

with too many figures that take the viewer's attention away from Mazeppa and the horse. His literary inspiration seemed to have taken hold of him and the painting turned out to be more an illustration.

Baudelaire, alluding to Boulanger's painting in "Aesthetic Curiosities of the Salon of 1845," makes the point that "these are the last ruins of ancient romanticism—that is what comes of a time when inspiration sufficiently replaced the rest." [27] In other words, inspiration is all that commends the painting and little remains to be said about the work itself. Boulanger's painting, though not a great one, had a cultural and almost political significance for the development of French Romanticism, because it announced the triumph of Romanticism in art, for which the first impetus had been Géricault's *Raft of the Medusa*, and because it was the first visualization of the Romantic hero, accepted and interpreted as such, by the French. Mazeppa was France's Werther, its Childe Harold. Once this was established, Hugo could put on the finishing touches— very important ones. This painting, Hugo's *Les Orientales* and his "Preface" to *Cromwell*, with Ste.-Beuve's *Discours sur la littérature au XVIe siècle*, established French Romanticism firmly, and after them, *Hernani* and *Chatterton* could come. [28]

In the introductory remarks to *Les Orientales*, Hugo gives Boulanger high praise, calling him an artist of the first rank who is able to raise "our" school to the magnificent heights of the Italian, Spanish, Flemish, and English Schools. He dedicated two ballads to Boulanger: "Mazeppa," which served to inspire Hugo somewhat, and "Le Ronde du Sabbat," a response to Boulanger's "gigantic" lithograph. [29] Boulanger's painting of Mazeppa acted in a general, inspirational way upon Hugo's imagination, but there is really little direct correlation between the paint-

---

[27] Charles Baudelaire, *Oeuvres complètes* (Paris, 1961), pp. 827–28.

[28] Boulanger did other studies of Mazeppa, though *Le supplice de Mazeppa*, sometimes called *Le départ*, was the most famous. There are two lithographs called *Mazeppa, le départ*, that are slight modifications of the *Supplice*. There are a painting and two lithographs of *Mort du Cheval de Mazeppa* and two different proofs of lithographs entitled *Mazeppa dans le forêt*. See *Notes of the Catalogue Musée Fabre, 1914*. A study for *Le départ* is to be found in the Monteplier Museum. See also Aristide, p. 24, for *Mort du cheval de Mazeppa*. They are very reminiscent of Delacroix's and Vernet's work on the same subject, which reinforces my belief that Boulanger's work on Mazeppa was derivative to a large extend.

[29] *Les Orientales*, ed., Elisabeth Barineau (Paris, 1952), pp. 5–12.

ing and the poem. As Delacroix said, talking about literary work inspiring an artist, the imagination finds a subject in another art form that seems right for the expression of the artist's feelings and ideas in his particular mode of expression. Perhaps Boulanger's *Mazeppa* acted in this way at the most general level, but there were literary and other influences as well. The shadow of Byron's *Mazeppa* is cast on Hugo's poem, as is Hugo's own research on horses, done with the help of his friend the Orientalist Ernest Fouinet, and the performance of a mimodrama about Mazeppa at the Franconi's Cirque Olympique.

The importance of *Les Orientales* to the development of the French Romantic lyric has been pointed out many times, but what is rarely mentioned is that only two weeks before the book's appearance Count Jules de Rességuier published *Tableaux poétiques*, which was a great critical success and contained some of the same material that Hugo included in *Les Orientales*.[30] In the third edition, Rességuier added a poem about Mazeppa. Rességuier and Hugo rely heavily on Byron, but it is instructive to see how they differ in the treatment of the same subject. Even though Rességuier's "Mazeppa" came a little after Hugo's (the third edition came two weeks after *Les Orientales*), the *Tableaux poétiques* should be considered first, for these poems really explain a great deal about the literary milieu in which the more famous *Les Orientales* were published.

The title *Tableaux poétiques* itself suggests a concept of the rapport between poetry and painting. These poems are like canvases, and a reviewer of this volume for the *Journal des Debats* speaks of them in this way, saying that a young poetry has emerged in France whose point is "to paint the century and the society," whose real mission is not the imitation of nature but "the painting and explanation of the secret, intimate emotion without which one cannot write." In *Tableaux poétiques* imagination designs reality that renders in each detail "form" and "color." Real life returns there and is reflected there. The poetry of these tableaux is of "our" time; it speaks to the spirit and traces some scenes of our social existence with its illusions and colors. All that animates it.[31] Rességuier's

[30] There were five editions: January 5, 1829; March 9, 1829; late spring 1829 (augmented with *Mazeppa* and other poems); the spring edition was published again in 1829 as the fourth edition; 1838.
[31] In the *avis des éditeurs* to the fourth edition of *Tableaux poétiques* par le Cte. Jules de Rességuier (Paris, 1829), pp. i–iii, this review of the first edition is included.

poems contain some of the current, important ideas and literary vocabulary of the time: the painting of poetry, the symbolism of nature, the
local color of Walter Scott's novels, and the orientalism of Thomas
Moore's poems are all represented in this volume.[32]

Jules de Rességuier was from Toulouse, where he established his reputation as a good poet early in the nineteenth century. In 1819, Alexandre
Soumet, having achieved the Jeux-Floraux, considered him a great ally
in making this literary conquest. By 1820, he became friends with Hugo.
They spoke from time to time about literature and shared many of the
same ideas, so it is not surprising that they should be writing about the
same themes. In the case of "Mazeppa," it is tempting to suggest that
Rességuier wrote his after the publication of Les Orientales and was, perhaps, even inspired by Hugo's poem and the éclat Boulanger's painting
made in 1827. In 1828, the Mercure du XIXe Siècle, commenting on the
additon of "Mazeppa" to the Tableaux, says that "M. Boulanger inspired
two poets, and their inspiration took the form of the inspiration of their
turn of mind, lyric in one and picturesque and descriptive in the
other." [33] Boulanger's painting probably did inspire Rességuier's poem,
but overwhelmingly, Rességuier depends upon Byron.[34] The distinction
made by the reviewer between picturesque and descriptive on the one
hand and lyric on the other is a good way to begin to discuss these two
works.

Rességuier's quotation from Voltaire's Histoire de Charles XII is almost
entirely the first citation Byron uses in his "Advertisement." He
also writes in couplets, as did Byron in Mazeppa. The poem is divided in
half: the first 46 lines deal exclusively with the horse, the last 46 with a
monologue by Mazeppa and a description of his rescue by a Tartar girl.
Although the poem is in many verbal ways close to Byron's, there are
significant differences of conception. Rességuier does not set the scene
for the flight across the steppes; he, like Hugo, begins the poem after the
ride has started, and like the artists before him he takes this episode for
his focus. The opening lines could in so many ways apply both to Mazeppa and his horse:

[32] Important poems are: "Le source des Montagnes," "Le Pélérin imité de Walter Scott,"
"L'Odalisque," "Le Schall," "Chant Oriental imité de Thomas Moore," "Le Punch."

[33] Mercure du XIXe Siecle 24 (1828): 417.

[34] Joseph Dédieu, "La Poésie de Jules de Rességuier," Les Annales Romantique: Revue
d'Histoire du Romantisme 10 (1913): 82–84.

> Jeune fils indompté des forêts de l'Ukraine,
> Egalent dans son vol la rafale Africaine,
> Il fuit, et son beau corps par l'écume est blanchi.

But that fusion quickly disintegrates. Attention is turned to the speed of the ride. The horse is driven to this frenzy because "Son coeur est appelé vers de lointain rivages." From lines 11 to 26, the poem is a series of questions and answers. The narrator is naive, in a way that mars the poem. What is that moving burden on his back? One cannot tell because the horse is moving so fast. Where does he come from? Where is he going? These are the sort of questions Ryleev asks in *Voynarovsky*, but in this case most of them remain unanswered. Then follows a statement: out of the heart of the whirlwind rises a plaintive cry. Is that the groan of a human voice or the horse's neighing? The questions become coy and cloying, but one sees that Rességuier was trying, though unsuccessfully, in these questions to achieve rhetorically a sense of speed and mystery. The first 26 lines try to give the impression of a horse rushing from the background, where the sound of its hoofs can scarcely be made out, to the foreground; the effect is as if the narrator were standing still and the horse were approaching him. The horse falls dead quite dramatically, and we then learn that his burden is a young man. It is as though one were given all the action before the moment Delacroix chose to paint the death of Mazeppa. Rességuier's effect is that of a sequence in a motion picture that ends with a freeze frame. He lets the reader know that he is definitely speaking about the horse at the opening because lines 27–30 are set off and inform the reader:

> Et sur son corps fumant, sur son flanc ateré,
> Un jeune homme tout nu, tout sanglant, déchiré,
> Contre l'étrat lien qui l'enchaîne immobile
> Essayant les efforts d'une rage inutile.

What follows is a description of the horses that suddenly appear in section XVII of Byron's poem. Now the narrator sees them perfectly well and relies heavily upon Byron's description. The narrator makes it clear that he and the reader are going to overhear Mazeppa's monologue. Lines 46–76 are the dramatic center of the poem, and contain essentially the same story that Byron tells. What is wrong about Rességuier's monologue is that it goes against all reality; the lurid remarks by Mazeppa could hardly come at the time they do. Byron realized this and had his Mazeppa speak years after the event. Rességuier's immediacy seems foolish. He tries to get the monologue to move toward unconsciousness by introducing a hallucination at the end where Byron introduced the dream.

> A l'heure où nous quittons ce monde passager,
> On dit que plein d'amour, un divin messager
> Se repare pour nous de la sainte phalange,
> Et qu'à l'instant suprême on aperçait un ange:
> Et déjà devant moi les cieux semblent s'ouvrir.
> Oui, le voilá cet ange! il vient, je viens mourir.

Up to this point Mazeppa has filled in the details of how he ended up bound to this horse. Rességuier has added a Christian touch to Byron's closely psychological analysis of almost dying that seems a little out of place and out of character. One does recall that Mazeppa said in Byron's poem, section VII, "My moments seem'd reduced to few;/ And with one prayer to Mary Mother,/ And, it may be, a saint or two, . . ." but if Rességuier had this in mind he missed the irony of it. The whole scene of moving into unconsciousness falls flat in Rességuier's poem because it is a mere description.

The last section, lines 77–92, is also descriptive. A young Tartar girl, finding Mazeppa unconscious, is frightened but decides to help him. Mazeppa does not revive in the poem; the narrator merely comments:

> Et ne se doute pas, dans son naif effroi,
> Qu'à son peuple guérrier elle prépare un roi.

Rességuier made an obvious historical error, for Mazeppa did not become Khan of the Tartars; but he did in a mimodrama entitled *Mazeppa ou le cheval Tartare, mimodrame en trois actes* by Jean Cuvelier de Trie and Leopold A. Chandenson with music by Sergeant.

The equestrian play was first performed on January 11, 1825, with Adolphe Franconi, of the famous family of trick horse riders, as Mazeppa. The Cirque Olympique was extremely popular and was attended not only by the French but also by hundred of Europeans passing through Paris. The Franconis and their daring horsemanship were well known by Hugo and the *cénacle*. The Mazeppa in the mimodrama is barely connected to any historical concept of the Ukrainian Hetman. A good indication of what it was like appears in a notice in a Warsaw paper, *Monitor Warszawski,* only a couple of weeks after it premiered in Paris. "The author makes the hero the son of the Tartar Khan, taken as a child to Poland, where he fell in love with a magnate's daughter. He kills his rival, but they catch him, tie him to a wild horse that carries its rider over the steppes to his father's territory. The old Khan gives his son his land and power; the son then returns to Poland. There are storms and deserts, and finally he plunders and burns the castle where his loved one lives. He forces his father to allow her to marry him. The ceremony takes place by the fire of a huge pine tree." [35]

The emphasis in such a presentation would of course be in the trickery with the horse; the spectacle is what counted. Rességuier's poem transforms the visual qualities of the Cirque Olympique's production into verbal ones; he relies mostly upon Byron's poem rather than the mimodrama text, except for such slips as making Mazeppa a Tartar Khan. Probably the most interesting aspect of the poem is Rességuier's attempt to create a sense of movement in poetry as he saw it at the Cirque Olympique. The twentieth-century metaphor for the technique is cinema. The poem ends with an unhappy abruptness without the action's being resolved. The sudden ending is reminiscent of Byron's terse conclusion to *Mazeppa,* but Rességuier's poem remains purely descriptive without a hint of Byron's symbolism.

Hugo's "Mazeppa," however, is a poem of another order. Coming as it does at the end of a series of artistic works about Mazeppa, it is almost fitting it should surpass them. One feels Hugo is almost consciously demonstrating that the subject can be made symbolic if handled properly. The poem, like Rességuier's, is divided into two parts: Part I is

---

[35] Raszewski, pp. 406–7. This equestrian drama has an interesting history that shows how wide the Mazeppa theme spread. John Howard Payne, the American actor, reworked the Leopold-Cuvelier drama into *Mazeppa, or the Wild Horse of Tartary,* an equestrian melodrama in three acts for production in America. It is in the Harvard Theater Collection. See John Howard Payne, *Trial Without Jury & Other Plays,* eds. Cadman Hislop and W. R. Richardson (Princeton: Princeton University Press, 1940). The editors note also, p. 165, "According to the contemporary review in *The Drama,* the anonymous *Mazeppa; or the Wild Horse of the Ukraine,* which was acted in November 1823, at the Royal Cobourg, but which has not been preserved in either manuscript or printed form." According to Borschak, the Leopold-Cuvelier was plagiarized as *Mazeppa ossia il cavallo selvaggio* in Venice in 1838. And finally, it was redone by P. C. Arnault as *Mazeppa ou les revoltes de l'Ukraine. Pantomine à grand spectacles en 3 actes et 5 tableaux* in Paris in 1857.

Hugo's recapitulation of Byron's poem and Boulanger's painting, and Part II is his symbolic creation.

The poem has an epigraph from Byron ("Away!—Away!—") and begins by describing the scene of Boulanger's *The Agony of Mazeppa*. Mazeppa is raving and crying and the horse is in a fury. The visual and auditory impression is of restraint of a great deal of energy that when released will move like a bullet. Pain, tension, and fury are controlled until line 13—"un cri part . . ."—where horse and rider are off across the plain. They move across the shifting sands, filling a whirlwind with noise, like a black cloud full of thunder and lightning; they fly with the winds. Hugo has condensed the 105 lines of Byron's sections IX, X, and XI into 18. One can see the words and phrases that Hugo must have fallen upon whether in English or in French: "wild," "snorting," "struggling," "full foam of wrath," "sudden lash," "my breath was gone," "savage shout," "upon the pinions of the wind," "we sped like meteors through the sky,/ When with its crackling sound the night. . . ." These are the violent, vivid images that Hugo fused into his own eighteen lines. Boulanger's painting, acting in conjunction with these words and phrases, probably helped serve as inspiration for these lines.

At line 19 and for the next twelve lines Hugo amplifies the images of speed and space. This is a particularly good section of the poem in which to analyze how he enriched and concentrated Byron's materials. The lines from *Mazeppa* are:

> Away, away, my steed and I
> Upon the pinions of the wind,
> All human dwellings left behind.
> We sped like meteors through the sky,
> When with its crackling sound the night
> Is chequer'd with the northern light.
> Town—village—none were on our track,
> But a wild plain of far extent,
> And bounded by a forest black . . .
>
> (XI, 422–31)

Byron's sections are first of all not divided into stanzas but into verse paragraphs. The fairly regular iambic lines and rhyming couplets give a natural order to the sense of the words. He is not playing with rhythm at all, but of course he is somewhat held to the frame of his poem, which is a narrative, for Mazeppa is telling about an event in the past. It could be, and sometimes is, a dramatic monologue.

Hugo's narrator is there: sometimes objective, sometimes so caught up in the events that his excitement colors his view. Hugo wrote the whole poem in a six-line stanza that is actually a pair of tercets (the first two lines are Alexandrines; the third is a six-syllable line) joined by a rhyme in the third line of each. Sometimes the lines enjamb, sometimes they are end-stopped. He obviously has the shortened ballad line in mind here and uses it to create a number of auditory effects. The lines are:

> Ils vont. Dans les vallons comme un orage ils passent,
> Comme ces ouragans qui dans les monts s'entassent,
>   Comme un globe de feu;
> Puis déjà ne sont plus qu'un point noir dans la brume,
> Puis s'éffacent dans l'air comme un flacon d'écume
>   Au vaste ocean bleu.
>
> Ils vont. L'espace est grand. Dans le désert immense,
> Dans l'horizon sans fins qui toujours recommence,
>   Ils se plongent tous deux.
> Leur course comme un vol les emporte, et grands chênes,
> Villes et tours, mont noir liés en longues chaînes,
>   Tout chancelle autour d'eux.

Hugo builds simile upon simile in the first three lines: storms become tornadoes become a ball of fire. Byron's "upon the pinions of the wind" and "We sped like meteors" seem flat in comparison because they state rather than render the movement; Byron extends the simile in a classical fashion and Hugo telescopes it. The color and energy of "meteors," "crackling sound," and "northern lights" are brought together in Hugo's one image of "ball of fire." The next three lines suddenly move the reader from the massive to the minuscule. Horse and rider are only a dot in the fog, not unlike the size of a meteor when one sees it in the sky. Rességuier tried to get this same effect of great distance, but he merely led the reader to it while Hugo's jumps to it in a flash. The man and horse are like a bit of foam on a vast ocean; another short simile to reinforce the first. Water, fire, energy, movement are all implications of these images in his similes.

Where Byron uses "Away, away," Hugo uses the flat statement, "Ils vont." In the next stanza this is followed by another simple statement:

"L'espace est grand." But from an initial, stationary point the stanza takes off. The horse and rider "plunge" into the horizon that is endless and recommencing. The speed of the world turning becomes the speed of the horse. Byron's "wild plain of far extent" turns into a real sense of immense space in Hugo's images of speed operating over space. In the same way Byron's "Town—Village—. . . wild plain . . . forest black" are put into motion in Hugo's last tercet in that stanza. In this section of the poem, Hugo is constantly striving for a sense of speed, to give the lines themselves greater motion. Byron does not get this sense in his lines, even though Mazeppa, when telling his story, moves into the historical present, creating a sense of immediacy of event. So much of the first section of Hugo's poem is like what one could have seen at Franconi's equestrian circus. For instance, in the last tercet quoted above, one feels as if a backdrop were whizzing by while in the foreground a horse and rider gallop on a conveyor belt. Hugo more successfully creates a moving picture in the mind of the reader than Rességuier and in the first part of the poem is often theatrical in the spectacular images he creates. That quality has often been called lyric, but at least in this poem it might be called "Circus dramatic." Hugo saw or heard about Franconi's daredevil riding in the Cuvelier-Leopold mimodrama, and probably had it in mind as he read Byron's poem and looked at Boulanger's painting.

The image of painting is continued at line 37; the moving backdrop blurs: "Tour voille et se peint de couleurs inconnues." More explicitly in this stanza than anywhere in the poem, Hugo creates the sense of a moving set being watched by a stationary observer. Mazeppa sees the trees, large clouds, the old ruined dungeon, and the mountains rush by. The lack of concentration of imagery in Byron's poem inhibits this same kind of response. At this point Hugo introduces the herd of foaming mares and wolves, both of which appear in Byron's poem and the last of which Boulanger painted in *The Death of Mazeppa's Horse*. Byron introduces the herd in section XVII to make the point that the horse had returned to its homeland to die, acting then as an analogue for Mazeppa's deliverance to his new country, the Ukraine. Rességuier merely describes the scene in his poem; there seem to be no personal or political implications. Hugo gives a picture of the herd of thundering horses and the flock of ravens pursuing the horse and rider across the plains as though these animals want to bring both of them down. The "cavales," however, are not only a reworking of Byron's material, but are also the introduction of a new source of inspiration. In the notes to *Les Orientales*, provided by and large by Ernest Fouinet, there is a long note to poem IX, "Nourmahal la Rousse," which includes Fouinet's translation of an Arabic poem entitled "La Cavale." [36] This poem is really a detailed description of a mare that probably influenced Hugo's image of the horse in "Mazeppa." The opening line has immediate overtones in the poem: "La cavale qui m'emporte dans le Tumulte a les pieds longs, les crins épars, blanchâtres, se déployant sur son front." [37] Instead of merely using this as a basis for his brief description of the horse in the poem, Hugo seems to have assembled all these physical characteristics and put them into motion into the speed and energy that Mazeppa and animal exhibit. He chooses to expend his descriptive energies on the body of Mazeppa and on the ravens.

The ravens are an expression of a few lines in Byron's poem and an interpretation of the birds that appear in Boulanger's painting. These five ravens are about to attack the writhing body of a helpless Mazeppa in the painting, but Hugo adds the eagle, the osprey, owls, and the vulture who circle "la funèbre volée." They have left the isolated oaks and their nests in manor houses to follow Mazeppa. After three days the horse falls dead, and Hugo gives a vivid description of the thousands of birds swarming over a nearly dead Mazeppa who is screaming and dragging himself along. This scene is dramatic and filled with Baudelairean ugliness and violence. The horse falls on a rock, cracking it while the birds scream above horse and victim. Mazeppa lies naked and miserable, spotted with blood. The birds hover in a cloud, waiting to pick at his tear-filled eyes with their beaks. It is a scene of great anguish; a man is reduced to a crawling thing. This is the moment that Boulanger has tried

---

[36] René Martineau, "Ernest Fouinet et 'Les Orientales,' " *Mercure de France* (June 16, 1916), p. 653. Here is an excerpt from a letter of Fouinet to Hugo dated 2 juillet 1829. "C'est pour la réssuciter que je vien à vous. Je suis encore tout plein de votre superbe *Mazeppa* après avoir relu celui de Byron. Si j'avais le plaisir de vous trouver lundi, j'aurais ajouté au manteau rayé, que vous avez si bien ajouté à sa taile, une noble et puissante déscription de la cavale d'Amraekis, poète Arabe célèbre et contemporain de Mohamet. Je vais vous le transcrire ici; elle pouvait éveiller en vous d'autres traits à ajouter à ceux dont vous avez ennobli le coursier sauvage de Mazeppa. Cela va droit à vous et je vous crois vous admirerez." It seems that Hugo did use some of this poem.

[37] Barineau, *Les Orientales* 2:204.

to capture in the *Death of Mazeppa*, but Hugo pulls back. Suddenly, in the middle of line 92, the narrator shifts to an abstract commentary about Mazeppa's becoming Hetman and about his revenge, as though Hugo sensed that to go any further would have destroyed his effect, for more might have been sentimental and unbelievable. The narrator says that Mazeppa will seed the fields with unburied dead and thus indemnify the osprey and the vulture. A savage greatness will be born of this suffering; he will become Hetman. At the end of Part I, the reader is tempted to see political overtones in these remarks, but they seem more a deference to the historical information in Byron's *Mazeppa* and a way to move away from the descriptive in a logical manner. Had Hugo ended his poem here, this would have been a natural though abrupt conclusion; and if one were prone to reading into the poem, much could be made of the horses and birds as allegories for peoples and nations, with Mazeppa representing Napoleon. But Hugo went on to write Part II.

There he explicitly makes the horse and rider symbolic by abstracting an analogue for art and the artist from this historical figure. His analysis of the symbol is a work of art exploring artistic creation and the artist. The argument follows this way: when a mortal, in whom a god seems manifest, sees that he is tied alive to the back of Genius, an ardent charger, he fights in vain. In other words, the artist is bound to Genius and cannot escape, though he tries to. Genius carries the artist outside the real world where it breaks down all gates with its feet of steel. Genius is a Pegasus carrying the artist over the world into somber regions. A thousand impure spirits press the artist on his flight. Hugo implies that the whole society does not understand and appreciate the artist. He passes on wings of flame all the fields of possibility, the worlds of spirit, and drinks from the eternal river. In the stormy or starry night, his hair is mixed in the tail of a comet and he blazes on the forelock of the sky. By this time, Genius, the horse, and the artist who rides him are fused into one in the language of the poem. The tireless flight of Genius takes the artist out of the banal world to the horizon of the ideal. Here is a beautiful description of world-weariness. The real world is ennui, the ideal is genius. Hugo says that only the demons and angels know what it is to follow genius. The artist suffers, strange lights shine in his eyes, he is burned by sparks of passion, and cold wings batter his face at night; only the artist riding Genius knows these things. He follows exhausted:

He cried terrified. You pursue implacably.
Pale, exhausted, gaping, under your flight that
                                            overcomes him,
   He bends with fear.
Each step you take seems to dig his grave.
Finally, the end comes. . . . He runs, flies, falls,
   And rises king!

Genius carries Mazeppa to his kingdom and the Hetman has been transformed into an artist. The idea for making Mazeppa a poet may have
come to Hugo from Byron's *Mazeppa,* section IV, where he says, "Even I
for once produced some verses,/And sign'd my odes 'Despairing Thyr-
sis,' " but Hugo goes beyond the casual utterance in that poem to suggest
that the artist is king, much, perhaps, as Shelley considered poets to be
the "legislators of the world." It is in Hugo's final stanza that all the
ideas, still not coherent in any one image or symbol by the French
Romantics at this time, fuse into the grand symbol of Mazeppa-artist.
After this, of course, the works that came before Hugo's poem could be
reinterpreted in this light and even Byron's *Mazeppa* could be reread in
these terms.

   It has been said by a number of critics that Hugo's "Mazeppa" is symbolic, but few have demonstrated how. Its symbolism was first analyzed
by a contemporary reviewer of *Les Orientales* in *Le Globe,* and most of his
analysis is still pertinent. Hugo

begins with Mazeppa, paints his long punishment and triumph. One could say
that he did not want to do anything else; one would say so because that covers
three-quarters of his poem. He does not stop any longer than a moment, and,
suddenly, he is not content to write genius on the pedestal of his symbol. But,
insensibly, he animates, he spiritualizes this great physical image that he has described; he does not remake it or transform it, but he makes seen somehow the
interior, the soul. Thus, the statue of Pygmalion becomes Galatea without
changing form. It is no longer Mazeppa chained to his horse, running in the
desert. *Feet of steel* and *cold wings,* all the expressions that had been taken literally
return figuratively. All spiritual parts of the object that the artist contemplates
he now produces not abstractly, but under the same form of similar parts of
the images, as so many harmonious emblems that agree with one another between them. Thus operates the fusion of a moral idea in a physical image.[38]

Essentially, Hugo juxtaposes a rich physical description to a figurative
one, which Byron also attempted. The review makes one think that

[38] Hugo, *Oeurvres,* Poésie 1:791–92.

Hugo's poem operates like an imagist poem or a Haiku, where the physical and moral are distinct and must fuse in the reader's mind; but Hugo actually provides guidelines for the reader's imagination through the device of the telescoping simile, and on a large scale, he binds the mortal to the back of a horse that itself becomes Genius. The simile and metaphor form a bridge between the physical and the "moral," fusing them into a symbol.

Beginning with Byron's *Mazeppa* and culminating in Hugo's poem the same theme is being worked over in different degrees of symbolism, but it is only in Hugo's "Mazeppa" that one finds the symbol clearly realized. It is as though Mazeppa were gathering more and more legendary material about him, working and transforming in the imaginations of Byron, Géricault, Delacroix, Vernet, Boulanger, and Rességuier, and taking a final form in Hugo's conception of him. As it turns out, in the Western tradition, Hugo's Mazeppa is the culmination of the legend of the wild ride. It appears afterward in Europe and America, but it never surpasses Hugo's working of the material.[39]

Hugo clearly defined the suffering and triumph of the Romantic artist who was, for the French at least, the new hero. The horse, so often encountered in Romantic works of art, was given its new meaning: genius. The wild power, the mad speed, the sleek beauty of horse and man in French painting was given verbal form by Hugo. After Hugo's poem, the French had little to say about Mazeppa, but by then everyone in artistic circles knew what he symbolized. He was an artistic creation, acting as a declaration of the French Romantic artists that this is who they were: tortured geniuses, alienated from society, unknown by society, but coming to save it.

[39] In France afterward there were a few works in which Mazeppa appears, but they either copy Byron or recall Hugo. In 1830 in Paris an anonymous novel was published: *Mazeppa, chef des Cosaques de l'Ukraine. Roman historique sous le règne de Pierre le Grand, impér. de Russie et Jean Casimir, roi de Pologne.* I have not been able to locate this novel, but it may be the same as one published in London, also anonymously, in 1850, *Mazeppa, or, the Wild Horse of the Ukraine.* The latter is highly episodic and includes much fictional material. A lithograph of Mazeppa by Leroy was published in *L'Artiste* in 1830, too. Mazeppa is also mentioned in Petrus Borel's *Madame Putiphar* (Paris, 1839). Théodore Chassériau did a painting of Mazeppa in 1851.

4.

EAST EUROPEAN SOURCES
OF THE MAZEPPA LEGEND

ONE MUST TURN BACK to the seventeenth century to see how the legend developed in Eastern Europe before considering the relation of the two in the works of Ryleev, Pushkin, and Słowacki. From the start Mazeppa had a different significance in the Ukraine, Poland, and Russia, for he was, after all, born in that part of Europe and his life made an impact upon the territorial and political destinies of those countries. Often, the details of the lives of men who come seemingly from nowhere into prominence are vague. Historians may be frustrated by the paucity of factual material, but other men—historians as well—all possessing some measure of myth- or legend-making imagination, often help to generate a legend by adding speculation and opinion to the few facts. A historical figure like Mazeppa—whose origins, youthful experiences, unusual rise to political power, dramatic defeat, and death in exile, are mysterious—naturally lent himself to such legendary treatment.

Even in the light of twentieth-century scholarship Mazeppa's life before he became Hetman on August 4, 1687, remains sketchy.[1] He was born in either 1632 or 1644, and was probably descended from the lower Ukrainian gentry. As a young man he was a page in the Polish Court of Jan Kazimierz, but there is no substantial account of his life there. After

[1] The general historical information in this chapter is based upon: W. E. D. Allen, *The Ukraine; a History* (Cambridge, England: The University Press, 1940); Bohdan Kentrschynski, *Mazepa* (Stockholm, 1962); Borys Krupnyckyj, *Geschichte der Ukraine von den Anfagen bis zum jahre 1917* (Wiesbaden, 1963); *Hetman Mazepa und seine Zeit (1687–1709)* (Leipzig, 1942); Clarence A. Manning, *Hetman of the Ukraine: Ivan Mazeppa* (New York: Bookman Associates, 1957); *The Story of the Ukraine* (New York: Philosophical Library, 1947); Oleksander Ohloblyn, *Hetman Ivan Mazepa ta jaho doba* (New York: Organization for the Defense of the Four Ukrainian Freedoms, 1960).

an unspecified time at Court, Mazeppa left and seemingly disappeared;
however, about ten years later, in the 1670s, he appeared in the Ukrainian army. Why he left the Court and what he actually did in those ten
years are not known. The story, based upon the *Memoirs* of Jan Pasek
and the manuscript of an anonymous writer, is that he had an affair with
Countess Falbowska at the Polish Court, and her husband banished him
by having him tied naked to a wild horse that was let loose on the
steppes. There is reason to believe that Pasek made up this story to im-
pugn Mazeppa's character in revenge over a disagreement they had.

The story of his later life, his tenure as Hetman, his involvement with
King Charles XII of Sweden and Czar Peter I in the Battle of Poltava are
all well documented, yet no one interpreting that information can be sure
of Mazeppa's personal and political motives. He seems to have played off
all the people around him. While secretly negotiating with the Poles, he
was sending messages of allegiance to Peter I and hammering out the details of an alliance with Charles XII. He may have been honestly trying
to create a free Ukraine by using Machiavellian ploys to achieve his ends,
or he may have been siding with the country that would assure him the
greatest political power. Perhaps he was doing both. Whatever his grand
plan may have been, it did not succeed, for he and Charles XII were defeated by Peter I at Poltava in July 1709. Both had to flee to Bender in
Moldavia, where Mazeppa died in October 1709. The Battle checked
Charles XII's plans for conquest of Northern Europe and strengthened
Peter I's reign while it sealed the fate of the Ukraine for two centuries.
Just what Mazeppa was trying to accomplish then is not clear today, and
the picture of him that emerges now, when a great deal more historical
material is available than at the beginning of the nineteenth century, is
still filled with odd shadows and uncertain colors.

Even from such a sketch of Mazeppa's life one can see that his character and motivation lent themselves to conjecture, which is what happened in Eastern as well as Western Europe. Those siding with Peter I,
either because they were Russian patriots or because it was politically expedient, labeled him a traitor. Peter I was so personally angered by
Mazeppa's betrayal that he began in 1708—when he learned of the alliance with Charles XII—a campaign to wipe Mazeppa and everything
connected with him off the earth. Baturyn, Mazeppa's capital, was
burned to the ground, Mazeppa's name was pronounced anathema in all

Russian churches, he was accused of betraying the Russian Orthodox Church by intriguing with the Roman Catholic Poles, his name was removed from buildings, and artistic representations of him were destroyed wherever found. Peter's personal revenge hardened into official Russian policy, so that through the nineteenth century and up to the 1917 revolution, any history written under the aegis of the Russian Government that dealt with Mazeppa had to portray him as a traitor.

A second view of him was taken by the men who believed Mazeppa was secretly struggling to free the Ukraine from Russian oppression. His close friend Filip Orlik became the unofficial Hetman after Mazeppa's death and headed the first Mazeppist group that began a rather ineffectual underground movement for Ukrainian independence. To those people Mazeppa was a kind of revolutionary hero who had to use every kind of deception to try to achieve the desired political ends. In their eyes he was inspired by freedom and believed that anyone, including himself, could or should be sacrificed to the greater cause of liberty. For them he became an ideal liberator, a refined version of the Noble Outlaw, or— more appropriate to the Eastern European mind—a version of the patriotic traitor. His treachery or his revolutionary patriotism becomes the core of his legend in the Romantic art of Eastern Europe, and artists with partisan political ideas use Mazeppa either to prove a historical point or to convey their personal political feelings. Słowacki's play about Mazeppa, of all the Ukrainian, Polish, and Russian works about him, lifts the theme from politics and history onto a spiritual plane.

Mazeppa's legend in Eastern Europe, however, actually begins during his hetmanate and is reflected in the extant works of art about him from the 1690s and early 1700s; although the majority praise him, there are a few that indicate that he was not loved by all his people. The first known reference to Mazeppa in any art form appears in a panegyric "The Roxolanian Muse, about the Triumphant Fame and Fortune of Hetman Mazeppa," written in Polish by the Ukrainian poet Ivan Ornovsky in 1688, about a year after Mazeppa became Hetman. The poem extols the Hetman's virtues. Included in the text is an engraving of the Hetman by an obscure Ukrainian artist, Ivan Shchersky, and Mazeppa's coat of arms.[2]

---

[2] There is a portrait of someone who might be Mazeppa in the Monastery of the Caves in Kiev that antedates Shchersky's, but I omit discussion of it, agreeing with the argument that "it is impossible to believe that Czar Peter would have left this picture of his most

Between 1689 and 1698, Shchersky engraved at least four coats of arms with a likeness of Mazeppa; they were added to serious philosophical works, panegyrics, or statements of fealty to the Hetman. For instance, Shchersky's Mazeppa coat of arms can be found on the title page and scattered throughout the text of the first book in honor of Mazeppa, Stefan Yavorksky's *Echo of a Voice Crying in the Wilderness* (1689). The author became Patriarch of Moscow in 1702.

Yavorsky's book, which contains a six-stanza epigraph, ten Polish poems, a cycle of Latin poems, and a prose epilogue, praises the past and present of Mazeppa and the House of Mazeppa [3] by linking him to most of the great classical gods from Apollo to Mars. In 1690, Yavorsky wrote a Latin panegyric dedicated to "the most Magnificent and Illustrious Lord Johan Mazeppa, Leader of the Army," a Biblical allegory treating Peter I as Absalom and Mazeppa as King David.[4] More of the same kind of praise was written by Filip Orlik in "The Russian Alcides, Crowned with the Triumphal Laurel," written in a mixture of Polish and Latin and celebrating in allegory Mazeppa's seizure of a strategic fortress on the Sea of Azov. What is most important about both Yavorsky's and Orlik's works as concerns Mazeppa's image is the allegorical treatment of him in Christian and pagan terms and the juxtaposition of Mazeppa to great men and events of the past, explicitly calling attention to his own greatness.

Probably the most important work of art to appear about this same time was Leontii Tarasevich's allegorical portrait of Mazeppa in 1695.[5] It

---

hated friend in the most sacred church of Russia." Kentrschynskyi, p. 203. For Ornovsky's poem see Mykhalo Maksymovych, *Sobronie Sochinenii*, 3:715. Ornovsky wrote another work in honor of Mazeppa, *The Theater of Perpetual Glory* (Chernihin, 1699), the text of which is not available.

[3] A copy of this book can be found in the Saltykov-Shchedrin Public Library in Leningrad under sygn. 13 VII. I 287. Excerpts in Ryszard Lużny, "Stefan Javorsky—poeta niezany," *Slavia Orientalis* 16, no. 4, pp. 369–70.

[4] I did not read this poem but relied upon the general description of it in Alfred Jensen, *Mazepa: Historiska Bilder Från Ukraina och Karl XII:s Dagar* (Lund, 1909), p. 219. According to him, a copy could be found in the Rjazan seminarienbibliotek at that time.

[5] Kentrschynskyi, p. 208. According to Dymytro Rovinsky, the engraver, collector, and engraving preserver, the painting was also engraved on "Okronomy Arkushy" and pasted into *Slava Shermetry*, for which Orlik wrote *Hippomenes Sarmacki*. Valodymyr Sitchynsky, "Graviury Mazepy: graviura na chest Mazepy i gravirovoni portrety Hetmana," *Mazepa: Zbirnik*, Prace Ukrainskiego Instytutu Naukowego 46 (Warsaw, 1938–39):192.

is a round portrait of a beardless Mazeppa—dressed in armor, cloak over his shoulders, mace in hand—resting on a cloud and held up there by the casual grasp of a group of classical deities and a trumpeting angel. Surrounding the portrait are the words *Hisce Securus* ("Fearless"). Below, on the ground, a goddess spreads flowers on the earth; she is in the right of the picture. In the left is a bearded angel, human in form but for his wings, casually resting his hand on an unusual small cart or wagon that might be there to carry the harvest of an allegorical garden that has produced strange fruits: keys, a ring, three maces, a sword, a flag bearing a two-headed eagle, a small chest, and two chalices. All of these are to be interpreted allegorically and can be seen to apply to Mazeppa's accomplishments, or as some believe, his aspirations: leadership, power, and virtues, both personal and cultural. The portrait is the first visual representation of the apotheosis of Mazeppa; Yavorsky's allegorical book and panegyric apparently had already exalted him as the embodiment of Apollo and King David in prose and poetry. This portrait, however, is embedded in a vastly larger background of allegorical material that connects the Hetman with the more-than-human. His portrait does not touch the ground; he is above the mundane and is supported by pagan gods and Christian angels. Of course, the elaborate mixture of real, allegorical, Christian, and pagan is part of the Baroque style, and in conventional ways this is just another Baroque portrait in which a ruler, because he was supposed to be endowed with divine right or inspiration, had to be represented as above the common man and in the company of the gods.

But in 1704, to choruses of praise begin to be added a few discordant notes. In the previous year Mazeppa's power as Hetman had been challenged by Semen Palia, a popular leader among the Ukrainian peoples who had gathered a small army to drive the Poles from the western bank of the Dnieper River. In the process he gained power and prestige because he seemed to be waging a war of liberation. Mazeppa, perhaps seeing Palia as a challenge to his own power, captured the rebel leader and convinced Peter I that Palia was in league with the Swedes and succeeded in having him banished to Siberia. On the immediate political level, such a move obviously strengthened Mazeppa's position, but it caused deep disaffection among the people because Palia appealed to the Ukrainians' aspirations for freedom, while Mazeppa, by siding with the

Czar, did not seem to have his peoples' wishes and welfare first in mind. Between 1704 and 1709 the people's disapproval surfaced in popular songs about the Palia affair, which were probably passed among them orally. Only sixteen such songs and their variants have been collected,[6] though there probably were more that never were recorded.

Almost all stress Mazeppa's duplicity and betrayal of Palia, as these lines, which occur in five of the songs, illustrate:

> Hey, come, come Semen Palia
> To my place for a banquet.
> Hey, Semen Palia, you won't get
> Any double dealing from me.[7]

They are ironic, for Palia did come in good faith and Mazeppa did have him captured and turned over to the Muscovites for disposal. The scene in almost all of these songs is the same: a banquet at which Mazeppa and Palia drink wine with honey, after which Palia is taken prisoner. In the versions written after 1708 Palia talks about Mazeppa's betrayal of the Muscovites to the Swedes, and none shows any sympathy for Mazeppa. They seem to be a natural outburst of anger by Palia's partisans, and indicate that before his betrayal of Peter I Mazeppa's personal and political motives had been called into question by his own people.

In 1705, shortly after the Palia affair, Feofan Prokopovich, Archbishop of Novogorod (an important ecclesiastical and academic figure in his day) published a tragicomedy, *Vladimir*, which in its Prologue and Epilogue praises Mazeppa as a great leader, a godly man, and a patriot. The mere association of Mazeppa with St. Vladimir, the first Christian ruler of Kiev, was prestigious.[8] The Epilogue alludes to "the Great Leader Mazeppa who will annihilate the haughty Swedish Lion." Of course, in three years Mazeppa was in league with that Lion. When Prokopovich threw in his lot with Peter I, however, after Mazeppa joined Charles XII, the Prologue was eliminated and the reference to him in the Epilogue was altered to "Christ's serf."

---

[6] Mykhal Drahomanov, *Politychne Pisni Ukrainskogo Narodu* (Geneva, 1883). He claims to have corrected errors and to have given most variants.

[7] *Ibid.*, p. 3.

[8] Feofan Prokopovich, *Sochineniia* (Moscow, 1961), p. 152; Vladimir Varneke, *History of the Russian Theater: Seventeenth through Nineteenth Century* (New York: Macmillan, 1951), p. 50.

The painter, Ivan Migur, surpassed Prokopovich's praises in a flattering portrait of the Hetman in 1706.[9] It is a very complicated picture that incorporates the allegorical and the realistic in a different way from Tarasevich, for the painting is composed of four levels. The lowest level consists of a scroll held at each end by two cherubs, above which is an elaborate version of Mazeppa's coat of arms. Directly above the crest stands Mazeppa dressed as a knight, holding a mace. He is flanked on both sides by figures representing his good works (religion, education, patronage of the arts) and his virtues (truth, justice, and goodness). Directly above Mazeppa is the figure of Christ as shepherd, and He is flanked on either side by three saints. Above Christ is another elaborate coat of arms and flanking it on both sides are three churches that Mazeppa had built. The portrait thus illustrates his cultural works and his personal virtues, while linking him closely to the Orthodox Church. The painting is to be interpreted by connecting the figures horizontally and vertically and by drawing unmistakable parallels between the virtues and saints and between Christ and Mazeppa, which go much further toward the deification of Mazeppa than previous works. Here Mazeppa is one among the saints. The coat of arms at the bottom is surrounded by the implements of war, and Mazeppa's feet are firmly planted in that base, but his warrior qualities are subordinated to his Knighthood in the Army of Christ.

Migur's painting illuminates some of Mazeppa's cultural qualities, which became a part of the Hetman's heroic aspect. He actually was a learned man who supported and encouraged early Ukrainian culture. Among his best known accomplishments Mazeppa constructed new churches and monasteries and rebuilt old ones; large financial and artistic contributions to the Kievan Academy reached their zenith during his reign; he donated a silver plaque to the Church of the Holy Sepulcher in Jerusalem; and he had the New Testament printed in Arabic. He could speak and write Latin, Church Slavonic, Polish, and Ukrainian, and had

---

[9] Sitchynsky, "Graviury, . . ." 142; Kentrschynskyi, p. 272. Also according to Sitchynsky, between 1691 and 1706 portraits of Mazeppa were done by Zakhary Samoilovich, but they are not to be found in Kiev and Moscow, where they were done. Kentrschynskyi reproduces two portraits: one done c. 1700, p. 224 (also reproduced in Jensen); and another done c. 1703. They may have been done by Samoilovich, but their dates and authenticity are dubious.

political and cultural contacts in the West. Although Eastern European artists in the nineteenth century hardly mention his cultural activities directly, almost all of them, even those who see him as a traitor, consider him a cultivated man.

His refined qualities and largesse should therefore not be underestimated, but must be regarded with the mysteriously sly side to his nature. In 1706, Mazeppa was carrying out a secret plan. He had managed to come through the personal and political turmoil of 1703–4 with Semen Palia without losing the confidence of Peter I, but he was beginning even then to negotiate through a Polish Princess and a Jesuit priest with Stanisław Leszcyński, still in power as the Polish King. Such dealings were a surreptitious challenge to Peter I, because the Czar upheld the rights of Augustus II to the Polish throne after Charles XII had forced him to abdicate and replaced him with Leszczyński. Mazeppa's political machinations at this time seem as intricate as a Byzantine mosaic.

Amid these negotiations with the Poles, Vasyl Kochubey and Ivan Iskra decided to discredit him in the eyes of the Czar. Kochubey may have had an ulterior purpose for wanting to slur the Hetman's character, because in 1704 Mazeppa had fallen in love with Kochubey's daughter Maria (Matrena). She was also Mazeppa's goddaughter and slightly more than one-fourth his age. Maria, against the wishes of her family, went to live in Mazeppa's home, but it is not certain that she became his mistress. The odd domestic situation created tension between Mazeppa and Kochubey, and was probably intensified when Maria was finally removed from Mazeppa's home by force and sent to a convent. The affair created a rift in the men's long friendship, and it seems likely that Kochubey never forgave Mazeppa this indiscretion.

Kochubey and Iskra passed information to Peter I that indicated Mazeppa had formed a conspiracy against him with Charles XII. Whether they knew this in fact or concocted the story is not clear, but they lost at their game and were eventually executed, while Mazeppa was reassured by the Czar that his loyalty was unquestioned. Mazeppa did in fact sign a secret treaty with Charles XII in 1708, after Charles attacked the Czar's armies in Lithuania, two years after the attempt to discredit the Hetman.

The year 1708 was also an important one for Mazeppa's reputation in art, but it is far different from the picture one gets from the historical

material. In that year the Arabic translation of the New Testament, subsidized by the Hetman, was published in Aleppo, Daniel Goliahovsky
completed a large painting with Mazeppa as its central figure, and Mazeppa himself allegedly wrote one important political poem and possibly
two others.

Goliahovsky's painting sums up in complicated detail Mazeppa's relation to the world.[10] He stands in the center with his right hand holding
up a larger-than-life-sized wooden cross—the same cross that appears in
his coat of arms. The viewer is supposed to connect Mazeppa to Christ,
but a little less obviously. In his left hand is his shield raised high. His
face is stern and unsmiling. Mazeppa is standing on a small island and
surrounding him are eight female figures (six on the left, two on the
right) representing his good works. The island is separate from the rest
of the background of the painting: castles are burning, towers are falling,
ships are sinking, and people are pleading for mercy. The whole apocalyptic scene is overcast with dark storm clouds. In the upper left-hand
corner are the Virgin and St. Joseph; this is the only intensely lighted
portion of the painting. In the storm clouds across the top is a banner,
held by an angel hovering over Mazeppa; it bears this quotation from
Horace in inaccurate Latin: "The weak world falls to ruin, upheld by the
dauntless destroyer." At the bottom is a long Latin inscription that epitomizes Hetman Mazeppa as the chief of the army, member of the illustrious Order of St. Andreas, protector of the church, and patron of the arts
during peace and war. The implications of the painting are that in the
midst of earthly turmoil, while Heaven looks on, Mazeppa is steadfast, a
man above the ordinary, a sufferer not unlike Christ; but above all, a
man on an island, alone. This painting does seem a fitting representation
of the end of his life when, be he traitor or hero, he was a man without a
country.

In general, paintings and portraits of Mazeppa up to this point give a
realistic depiction of the man, and allegorize or simply write out his spiritual and aristocratic virtues, linking him casually to the classical deities

[10] Wacław Lipiński, ed., *Z dziejów Ukrainy* (Kiev, 1912), pp. 635–38. There is also a
reproduction in Stychynsky, "Graviury, . . ." p. 149, but the former is much clearer. Jensen reproduces it, as does Kentrschynskyi, p. 289. Ohloblyn, pp. 387–88, says that the
painting was part of the Krasinski Library Collection in Warsaw and was destroyed in the
Second World War.

and emphatically to Christianity. He is mortal, but divinely inspired. In all these portraits Mazeppa seems not to take notice of all the allegory around him, be it Christian or pagan; he looks straight out from the canvas, neither touching nor being touched. Mazeppa is pictured as a man set apart from the rest of humanity, and what he appears to be is more important to his legend than what he was.

Mazeppa's legend is similarly enhanced by the poetry he allegedly wrote, especially "All Sincere Men Want Peace," a patriotic plea for Ukrainian solidarity that describes the political problems of the Ukraine in Mazeppa's time. This poem is not to be found in Mazeppa's handwriting, but is recorded in the papers of his friend and later enemy Vasyl Kochubey.[11] It could be that Kochubey wrote the poem to present as evidence against Mazeppa to Peter I; on the other hand, from what is generally known about Mazeppa's role as Hetman and his cultural interests, he himself could have written it. Whatever the case, the poem was used as evidence against him by the Muscovites and their allies.

The opening couplet is famous among Ukrainians: "All sincere men want peace,/ But all do not pull with one rope." There are those on the "right" and those on the "left," undoubtedly the banks of the Dnieper River, and they are their own worst enemies. In the next stanza Mazeppa asks his "brothers" to understand that the ship—the Ukraine—needs one helmsman to steer her—one Hetman. He speaks of the queen bee to which all drones give allegiance: "What a pity, God, that the Ukraine/ Will not group together for her sons." He tells how the people's loyalties are divided, how they are serving other masters—the Turks, Poles, and Muscovites—yet how all yearn for their motherland. The country has been beset from all sides; it has been burned and plundered. From all sides come insults calling the Ukrainians barbarians. "Why didn't you teach your brothers?/ Why did you let them leave to serve others?/ It is better to have struggled/ Together to fight off trouble." Mazeppa says that he cannot unify the country alone, and asks his generals and colonels to stop squabbling and to join him. They should

---

[11] The text, variants, and commentary are in Drahomanov, pp. 47–49. The other two poems are merely commented upon in Drahomanov. For the others see Hetman Ivan Mazeppa, *Pysannia* (Kharkov, 1943). For a translation into English of the first and second poems, see Vera Rich, "Two Poems of Hetman Ivan Mazeppa," *Ukrainian Review* 6, no. 3 (Autumn 1959): 46–48.

prepare firearms and sword, die for their faith, defend their freedom. Let glory reign; their rights will be won with the sword. The words are direct, strong, and rousing: the words of a troubled leader rallying his divided people to action.

The other two poems frequently attributed to Mazeppa add less directly to his patriotic image, but surely they helped to elicit more sympathy from his admirers. One is called "Oh, Misery, Misery," and presents the plight of the Ukrainians as a short bestiary tale. The young of a Lapwing are taken by Chumaks who drive away the mother. She begs them to return her young, but they refuse, so she wishes them continuing bad luck. The Chumaks represent the countries that have taken the Ukrainian young men into the army, and the Lapwing is the motherland begging for their return.

The third poem, "Poor is My Little Head," sometimes referred to as the "Psalm," begins with an orphan child asking: "Whom am I to turn to?" He answers his own question: "Jesus." The world, according to the orphan, is so filled with evil that the only sensible thing to do is to turn to God. In many ways this is a traditional religious poem expressing a man's disappointment with the world and the solace he finds in God, and if Mazeppa wrote it, the poem merely enhances his image as a lonely, religious man, like the portrait of him by Goliahovsky.

With the exception of the Palia songs, Mazeppa's image in art in his day was laudatory, but once he betrayed Peter I there was a sudden shift in feeling about him, and he was openly attacked, even by some of his former friends. Stefan Yavorsky, by 1708 a very powerful ecclesiastical figure in Moscow, not only pronounced the anathema at the Sobor Uspensky but also composed offensive poems about the Hetman,[12] and as pointed out earlier, Feofan Prokopovich eliminated references to Mazeppa in the Prologue and Epilogue to *Vladimir*. In 1708, however, the Kievan Academy dedicated to its great benefactor Mazeppa a thesis done by a young philosopher, Ivan Novytsky, under the direction of Prokopovich—shortly before Peter I's condemnation, no doubt. It seems only fair to Yavorsky, Prokopovich, and others who had changes of heart about Mazeppa to question the sincerity of their altered views. The wrath of the Czar could not go unnoticed or unsung, and for the sake of one's life

---

[12] Some examples are given in *Kievskaya Starina* 4 (July 1883): 592–96.

it would have been expedient to change one's mind about the greatness of the Hetman.

Immediately after Poltava some anti-Mazeppa songs were written in the Ukraine, but whatever scorn is leveled at Mazeppa seems to be tempered by various kinds of sorrow. The following is an excerpt from an anonymous song that appears to be a rousing, direct attack on the Hetman:

> Ah, treacherous John, Hetman Mazeppa!
> Why did you betray the Czar, His Majesty the Czar?
> What was it all about? Why wasn't it exposed?
> Honor? Fame? Or gold, was it?
> All those things are found in the earth and sea
> And on your estate. Was that too little for you? [13]

He is attacked on personal grounds for his spiritual and temporal greed, but people who knew anything about him in the Ukraine were aware of his generosity. Another song begins: "Mazeppa's fame, a headless name, what could you do?" [14] The poem goes on to list all the results of the defeat by the Muscovites: the Czar is still alive, the army is sad, Baturyn has been burned, etc. It laments the misery of the aftermath of defeat at Poltava, but contains less condemnation of Mazeppa than an implied condemnation of failure to defeat the Muscovites. This same note is struck in an old Swedish folk song of this time recorded by Alfred Jensen: "But what became of all the boasting? They [Mazeppa and Charles XII] did not get back to their land;/ They missed their armies and disappeared in Germany [sic]." [15] The post-Poltava poems seem to be attempts to praise with faint damning.

With the exception of these songs, there is no evidence that Mazeppa appears in any other work of art in Eastern Europe in the eighteenth century. One would like to agree with Eugène Vogué, an early-twentieth-century biographer of Mazeppa, in his rhapsodic projection of Mazeppa's legend into the eighteenth century:

Long before it inspired Byron, this epic about Mazeppa was sung under the trembling leaves on the banks of the Dnieper by blind poets who circulated among Ukrainian villages. These Homers of the steppes transmitted orally a whole cycle of legends attached to the figure of Mazeppa.

---

[13] Drahomanov, p. 50.   [14] *Ibid.*, p. 52.   [15] Jensen, pp. 218–19.

Such may have been the case, but unfortunately the epic and the cycle are unrecorded. What have come down to the present are some Cossack Chronicles written in the last part of the seventeenth century that began to circulate in the early eighteenth century and do mention Mazeppa. One is by an author who called himself *Samovidets* or Eye Witness, who describes incidents on the right bank of the Dnieper River with a sympathetic view of Mazeppa. A second, by Samiylo Velychko, Secretary General to Vasyl Kochubey, was completed by 1720; as one might expect, Velychko is hard on Mazeppa, calling him a Machiavelli and a sly fox. The third, published in 1742, was written by a Cossack who was among those elevated to nobility after the Swedish War, and his account shows no love for the Hetman. Most of these Chronicles slight Mazeppa in some way and center on the fame and fortune of his predecessor, Hetman Bohdan Khmelnytsky, probably the first leader to try to make the Ukraine an independent country.[16]

The general silence of the Mazeppa theme in art in the eighteenth century is not difficult to understand in light of the official Russian position toward the Hetman. Not unexpectedly, when the theme does make its appearance again in the early nineteenth century, the image of Mazeppa as a traitor is given a new face. In 1803, *Pułtawa; poemat epiczny* (*Poltava: Epic Poem*) by Nicodemus Muśnicki, S.J., was published in Poland. While extolling the virtues of Peter I, the poem is obviously an attack on Mazeppa. Ten cantos of conventional rhyming couplets describe the Battle of Poltava, and Muśnicki is quick to point out in his preface that everything is based on history: Voltaire, Lacombe, and Levéque. His description of Mazeppa in the poem places him squarely in the camp of those who considered him a traitor.

He was a statesman (the name Mazeppa is famous) whose heart was swelled with blind pride. He was a statesman prone to exaggeration from his youth; he was chased out of Poland because of a frivolous love affair in his youth. Everyone knows the story of that wretched, revengeful spectacle. The licentious youth was covered with tar and lightly sprinkled with feathers. Then he was tied to a wild horse's back and he was brought thus into the Ukraine where he sank into the life of the brawling Cossacks.[17]

[16] For a complete listing of Chronicles see Dmytro Doroshenko, *A Survey of Ukrainian Historiography* (The Ukrainian Academy of Arts and Sciences in the U.S., Inc.) 5–6 (1957): 1–435.

[17] Nicodemus Muśnicki, S. J., *Pułtawa; poemat epiczny* (Warsaw, 1803), p. 76.

It is interesting that this passage alleges that "everyone knows" about Mazeppa. Although it gives the impression that his name must have been quite common, there is nevertheless little artistic or historical evidence to support the claim. The passage is anti-Ukrainian as well as anti-Mazeppa; it picks up an old accusation by the Poles that the Ukrainians were barbarians. One recalls that Mazeppa himself, in his poem "All Sincere Men Want Peace," mentions this problem. To be sure, this attitude helped create a centuries-long tension between the peoples of these countries. It is fairly clear that in this passage Muśnicki has poetized Voltaire's paragraph about this episode and added the tarring and feathering, which he might have gotten from Pasek's *Memoirs*, if he saw them in manuscript. Later in the poem Peter I, presented as skeptical of human nature, says that he never really trusted Mazeppa anyway. Muśnicki not only excoriates Mazeppa, he also enhances the image of Peter I, which was his point in the first place.

Muśnicki's poem is in a sense a rebuttal to the Western legend of Mazeppa as embodied in Voltaire's *Histoire de Charles XII*, for he reiterates emphatically the official Russian view. In the second decade of the nineteenth century, however, in circles of Ukrainian historians and some Polish and Russian writers, that view was undergoing a subtle transformation; the Mazeppa theme gradually moved out of the history books and into literature. Just as Voltaire's *Histoire* became a major source of the Western legend, so an anonymously written history of the Ukraine brought the Eastern materials about Mazeppa into new forms.

Istoria Rusov (The History of the People of Rus) began to circulate in manuscript about 1820, and found its way through the intellectual circles of Eastern Europe in that form until 1846, when it was published.[18] It was the foundation of Dmitri Bantysh-Kamensky's four-volume *Istoria Maloi Rossii (The History of Little Russia)*,[19] which was pro-Russian and pro-Czarist but included a great deal of controversial historical material. In the 1830 and 1842 editions, Bantysh-Kamensky was able to acknowledge

[18] *Istoria Rusov ili Maloi Rossii.* See Elie Borschak, *La Légende Historique de l'Ukraine 'Istorija Rusov'* (Paris, 1949).

[19] *Istorija Maloi Rossii so vremen prisoedineniya onoi k rossiiskomu gosudarstvu pri tsare Aleksee Mikhailoviche, s kratkim obozreniem pervobytnoga sostayanya sego kraya* (Moscow, 1822). In that edition is an engraving of Mazeppa by A. Osipov. It can be found in vol. 3, p. 126 of the 1842 edition.

that his primary source was the *Istoria Rusov*, which is a subtle historical-political defense of an autonomous Ukraine. It speaks for all Ukrainians, while specifically addressing itself to the Ukrainian gentry that still preserved the customs and language. It seemed to whoever wrote it that the gentry were the only group that might effect a revival of interest in Ukrainian independence.

At the same time the *Istoria Rusov* idealizes the Cossacks, who were a separate group from the Ukrainians. They were wild brigand types who set up their own warrior organization, the Sich, in the fifteenth century, but were disbanded by the Empress Catherine and reemerged as a powerful element of Alexander I's army. In the Russian campaign of the Napoleonic wars, the Cossacks, as part of the Russian army, had won great acclaim as fighters. All of Europe knew about them, and when they came to Paris with Alexander I, they were admired for their ferocity, though not for their manners. The *Istoria Rusov* is filled with historical fact, which appealed to the Romantic adorers and imitators of Scott's historical novels, but it also had an emotional, political appeal that struck chords in Romantic minds and hearts. The line between fact and fiction was obscured. The Polish and Russian Romantics were often less interested in historical accuracy than in creating a sense of the present based on a remodeled past: a *zeitgeist*. Legend and history were a pleasing combination, and one sees among some Poles and Russians of this time that odd cultural phenomenon in which a legendary past is created to antedate and form a basis for history. Not having an *Iliad* or *Aeneid*, they wrote their own mythical past from folklore. They were inspired by the poems of Ossian and by Herder's idea of creating a national consciousness out of national myths. Elie Borschak, describing the *Istoria Rusov*, says it is *"un roman à thèse,"* because its purpose seems to be to create a sense of Ukrainian history with a legendary, emotional spirit.[20]

The *Istoria Rusov* is somewhat equivocal about Mazeppa.[21] The author quotes what Voltaire said about him but adds some information. According to the *Istoria*, Mazeppa was trained by the Jesuits in Poland.[22] This, though not true, supports part of the official view of him after Poltava that he was a traitorous Pole and a Papist. On the other hand, the author elaborates upon Voltaire's few sentences about Ukrainian in-

---

[20] Borschak, pp. 163–64. [21] Doroshenko, pp. 86–87. [22] Borschak, p. 152.

dependence, which more than balance the negative implications of some of Mazeppa's actions. Mazeppa's treason is considered an act of personal vengeance in return for the slap in the face that Peter I supposedly gave him at a banquet of Prince Menshikov during which Mazeppa asserted that the Ukraine should be an independent country. This episode, most likely apocryphal, found its way into Bertuch's play, Dorville's novel, ballads and songs, and Pushkin's *Poltava*. But the most important impression of Mazeppa in the *Istoria* is the text of a proclamation by him in 1708, promulgated after Charles XII entered the Ukraine and Mazeppa established his camp between Starodub and Novgorod-Siversk.[23] The text is not authentic, being the imaginative creation of the author of the *Istoria*; however, it is probable that Mazeppa did make some kind of declaration at that time, the text of which has not been found.[24] The fictional proclamation makes Mazeppa clearly a Ukrainian patriot, for in it he makes a plea for the freedom of the Ukraine as a sovereign, neutral state. The tone and subject matter of it are reminiscent of passages in Dorville's *Memoires d'Azéma* that deal with the same subject, a novel the author of *Istoria Rusov* was inspired by and used as a source of information. Whatever may be the case, this "history" became the new, authoritative basis for the Polish, Russian, and Ukrainian view of Mazeppa.

Bantysh-Kamensky's *Istoria Maloi Rossii* had to treat Mazeppa as a traitor because it had to pass the censors. It is an important work because it contains materials from the Moscow Archives that had not been available before, and the author has done a great deal of historical research that he is careful to document. He includes in his notes the letters of Mazeppa and Maria Kochubey, from which Pushkin would draw heavily for canto II of *Poltava*. These letters add a new dimension to the Hetman's character. His impulsive, youthful love is balanced by a new passion for a young girl in his old age. This affair is associated with Mazeppa's dispute with Vasyl Kochubey, Maria's father, and becomes a new focus of interest and a center for the accretion of new legendary materials about Mazeppa. In a sense, Bantysh-Kamensky introduced the Mazeppa theme to

[23] *Ibid.*, pp. 153–54.

[24] There is a document in the hand of Filip Orlik, dated 1712, that lists six articles of agreement between Charles XII and Mazeppa. It was found in the archives of the Château de Dinteville in 1922.

the Slavs officially, and after the theme is almost exhausted by the early 1830s, he published a *Zhizn Mazepy* (*Life of Mazeppa*) in Moscow in 1832 that was the final statement about the Hetman in Russian history for a long time.

The *Istoria Rusov* and *Istoria Maloi Rossii* were extremely important in the development of Mazeppa's image among Poles and Russians in the Romantic period. They supplemented Byron's *Mazeppa* but did not supplant it. Byron's version of the Hetman was not dismissed by them; they did, however, use this new material to try to give a more accurate historical picture of him. The result was to create their own legend, and it seemed unavoidable that as much as they tried to bypass Byron's Mazeppa, his image of the Hetman kept coloring theirs. At the root of the Romantic legend of Mazeppa in Poland and Russia is, of course, the earlier one generated about the time of his death that, in its basic form, conceived of Mazeppa as either a traitor or a hero and survived for over a hundred years. Slavic historians and writers seem to have chosen one of these views and generated new legends about Mazeppa based upon it.

From out of such historical material with whatever legendary overtones it acquired, Mazeppa again emerged into art, this time in the form of the *duma*, a kind of long lyric poem based on historical events in the Cossack Ukraine of the seventeenth and eighteenth centuries, which became a popular genre among Ukrainian, Polish, and Russian Romantics. The *duma* was one of the first forms for embodying historical material, in the way Scott's border Ballads and Schiller's *Balladen* dealt with such materials, and acted as a means of making the historical past meaningful and vivid to contemporary readers.

Julian U. Niemcewicz's *Historical Songs*, published in 1816, explains in the introduction the purpose of such songs and ballads and designates those on Ukrainian themes *dumy*. Part of Niemcewicz's statement of purpose is later quoted by Ryleev in his book of *dumy*, and clarifies the relationship between and aims of history and literature during the early Romantic period in Russia and Poland.

To remind the youth of the works of their ancestors, to make them familiar with the most wonderful epochs of their nations, to link love of country with their first imaginative impressions—it is unmistakably a chance to graft onto the people a strong attachment to their country: nothing in that time of first impressions, those early understandings, can be lost. They demand, with the years, the brave temper of war of defenders, and to the nation virtuous men.[25]

Such poems were meant to create a national consciousness and to prepare brave and virtuous young men and women, one assumes, to fight for that nation's independence. No doubt behind this view is Herder's *Volkslieder* (1778–79) and *Ideen zur Philosophie der Geschichte des Menschkeit* (1784–90) that laid down a program for reviving national feeling through schools, books, and newspapers using the national language. In his notes to the poems, Niemcewicz clearly considers the Ukrainians a separate people deserving of their own nation,[26] and Ryleev's *dumy*, published a few years later, make the point more strongly.

Bohdan Zeleski, the "Ukrainian Nightingale," as he became known in Poland, wrote almost exclusively about the Ukraine and often in the form of the *duma* or *dumka*, as it is called in Polish. In 1824, he wrote a *dumka* about Mazeppa.[27] The poem is after the fashion of Niemcewicz's "Historical Songs," with a long headnote and copious footnotes. Sources are mentioned and facts are corroborated, which give the whole an air of historical authenticity. Zaleski alludes to Jan Pasek's *Memoirs*, which he saw in manuscript, as a source for this poem. The headnote characterizes Mazeppa as "a somewhat wild character" with the "traits of his people." "He loved Polish girls but not Poles; he sang to the lute and longed for war." Although love and war were his passions, Mazeppa was also a poet; but, Zaleski adds, Hetmen were usually poets. Zaleski has in mind the poem Mazeppa allegedly wrote, and in general he tries to stress Mazeppa's culturally refined character. Zaleski compares Mazeppa to Bohdan Khmelnytsky, his predecessor and the originator of the idea of Ukrainian independence: both are called great fighters and poets. Zaleski, with Niemcewicz's remarks undoubtedly in mind, states his view of the relation of history, politics, and poetry in his headnote to the poem.

It could not be different in a warring nation and in one, loving before all else, its ancestors—to honor its fallen, national heroes and imitate them as well, or to be at once a warrior or a poet, that was the one superiority tolerated by the Zaporozhians.

[25] Julian Ursyn Niemcewicz, *Śpiewy historyczne* (Warsaw, 1816), p. 5.
[26] See expecially the song "Jan Kazimierz" and the notes to it. *Ibid.*, pp. 343 ff.
[27] Bohdan Zaleski, *Pisma Józefa Bohdana Zaleskiego* (Lvov, 1877) 1:135–42.

Here is the only instance in Slavic Romantic literature in which Mazeppa's poetry is linked to his heroism, but the combination of the poet and warrior was particularly appealing to the Romantics. Had not the poet-warrior Byron died at Missolonghi in 1824, the year in which this poem was written? There was an idea in some quarters of Europe in the 1820s that the artist, especially the poet, was by nature qualified to lead a nation. Zaleski's main interest, however, seems to be to give the reader a more accurate historical picture of the young Mazeppa, and from the headnote and the *dumka*, it is clear that Zaleski knows the history and literature about Mazeppa.

His *duma*, however, presents a totally fictitious situation to explain why Mazeppa left Jan Kazimierz's court. Instead of the tortuous ride, Zaleski uses a meditative one that evokes Mazeppa's patriotism. The young Mazeppa, with the Polish army, is near the town of Zamość where Khemelnytsky is commanding the Cossacks. His Ukrainian patriotism fired, Mazeppa decides to join his countrymen.

The poem, a dramatic monologue, begins with Mazeppa's recalling having made all his farewells in Warsaw. Tired but still yearning to fight, he digresses to thoughts of the Polish girl he left behind and to his lute. Pondering, he says: "Somewhere far, among the Ruthenians/ He [Mazeppa] will find love and peace. . . ." Poland and the Court bore him, and he chides the nobles for their inquisitiveness about his love affairs. He tosses off: "Every pretty girl is the same to me." He is not frightened by the horses of the steppes; being a warrior, he knows both real and imaginary fear. His position at court will never amount to anything because he is not a Pole, so "Why should I be a page here, where somewhere else I can be a prince?" Besides, the Polish youth are decadent; they have forgotten how to fight. He would rather be Hetman of the Ukraine than a noble among nobles. Zaleski makes Mazeppa an ambitious political character who dreams of fighting in the old Cossack way: ". . . with fire, sword/ We'll cut down, burn and flay." There is an echo here of Mazeppa's own poem, rallying the Ukrainians to unite. He goes on to recall those Ukrainian-Poles who rallied the Cossacks in the sixteenth century: Kosiński and Loboda. They fought for the Lachs, a pejorative term for the Poles, and the Poles, in turn, have abused the Cossacks, cursed them, and never let them free. Zaleski seems intent upon detailing that rivalry, which creates an intense reaction in Mazeppa, for he realizes that the Poles are again chasing the Cossacks, this time Khmelnytsky. But he says Bohdan will move out tomorrow, "And the day after tomorrow the Poles will see the guest." He will inform Khmelnytsky of the Polish plans. He urges his horse on, wishing his Polish sweetheart well.

The poem is first of all an overt attack upon the Polish treatment of the Ukraine. It introduces an old rivalry that helped create general political instability in the Russian-Polish-Ukrainian sector of Eastern Europe. For centuries many Polish and Ukrainian nobles bickered over territorial rights. The resulting internal strife Russia could and did use to her advantage, for it prevented each country from solidifying its power, leaving Russia continually in control. More important, however, Zaleski's poem is the first Eastern European Romantic work about Mazeppa to use historical sources to try to change the treacherous image of the Hetman. His poem is also an indication of the turn of the Slavic mind toward the use of history in literature to create a national consciousness. For all his insistence upon history in *Mazeppa*, Byron uses it as a backdrop for his central theme of the death-in-life experience. The Poles and Russians, also relying upon history, make it, however, the center of their works about the Hetman. His personal life, though important, is almost always secondary to the political outcome of his actions. There is a sense in this and subsequent Polish and Russian works, as there is not in Byron's and Hugo's, that a historical point is being made. Whereas Voltaire was trying to instruct princes in his *Histoire de Charles XII*, the *Istoria Rusov* and Bantysh-Kamensky, among others, were attempting to determine who was the legitimate power in Eastern Europe, what were the legitimate nationalities, and who were the rightful rulers. The historians did not agree and often gave confusing interpretations. Mazeppa became a medium for such large political arguments and in the process his legend became politicized. Once again, as in his lifetime, there were artists ready to make a hero or villain of him, but now for very different reasons.

5.

RYLEEV, PUSHKIN, AND MAZEPPA

THE FIRST important writer to take up the Mazeppa theme after Zaleski was Kondraty Ryleev, a young Russian poet in St. Petersburg who passionately espoused the cause of Ukrainian independence. His passion was, as it were, a cover for his anti-Czarist feelings and his growing sense that there must be a revolution in Russia to destroy imperial oppression. He was in fact one of the liberal Russian intelligentsia who agitated in the 1820s for such an insurrection and took part in the ill-fated December Revolt of 1824, for which he and a few friends were finally executed. He died at thirty and became a martyr to those liberals who survived Nicholas I's purge of the Decembrist rebels. The last important work he published was *Voynarovsky*, which was considered a seditious poem by the Czarist regime in 1825, but which now enjoys fame in Russia as one of the first pieces of literature to prefigure the Revolution of 1917. Its author became one of the first martyrs of the Proletarian Revolution.

Voynarovsky is the culmination of Ryleev's thinking about Mazeppa, for he had dealt with the Hetman in his *dumy* and in a sketch of a play about Mazeppa. When one goes back to those earlier works, one is struck with Ryleev's change of heart about Mazeppa over a few years, for at first the Hetman is clearly a traitor in the poet's eyes. Ryleev's change of attitude parallels to some extent his growing commitment to the revolutionary movement in Russia as he was exposed to more and more liberal-radical ideas and people. Many of his ideas were shaped by such works as *The History of the People of Rus*, Bantysh-Kamensky's history of the Ukraine, Karamzin's *History of the Russian Nation*, Niemcewicz's concept of history-literature, and the impact of Byron's life and poetry upon him. Of the people he talked to about the political-historical implications of literature, perhaps the conversations with Adam Mickiewicz and Antoni Malczewski, both poets exiled from Poland at the bidding of the Czar, were the most influential. Oddly enough, all of these influences were at work on Pushkin when he wrote *Poltava*, yet he interpreted them differently to reach conclusions antithetical to Ryleev's about Mazeppa.

Voynarovsky is essentially Ryleev's political credo; however, the often-quoted line from the introductory poem dedicated to Alexander Bestuzhev is at once a political and artistic manifesto if the whole statement is considered: "You will not find art here—/ But you will find live feeling—/ For I am a citizen, not a poet." [1] It was a daring declaration for Ryleev to make, one that his compatriots would quote long after his death. Before Ryleev came to his conclusions about the poet and his art and before he saw Mazeppa as a revolutionary leader against Russian Czarist oppression, he underwent some important changes in ideas about history, patriotism, politics, and Mazeppa, yet once Ryleev's political ideas crystallized, he saw affinities with Mazeppa's and embodied them in *Voynarovsky*.

Although his *Dumy* and *Voynarovsky* appeared in 1825, they had been read in salons and some parts were published in newspapers and journals between 1822 and 25. [2] What perhaps prompted Ryleev's literary interest in the Ukraine was Bantysh-Kamensky's *History of Little Russia* in 1822, and a trip he took into the Ukraine (Kharkov, Romnach, Kiev) in June and July 1822; in addition, he was of course familiar with the literary material on the Ukraine coming from Poland, and his friend Orest Samov was publishing a journal, *The Ukrainian Herald*, at the University of Karkov. In the last half of 1822, Ryleev began to sketch a tragedy about Mazeppa. Considering the cast of characters, the scenario, and some of the speeches, it becomes apparent that Ryleev was more interested at that time in Mazeppa's alleged love affair with Maria Kochubey and with his relations with Kochubey and Iskra than in politics; but for

---

[1] Kondraty F. Ryleev, *Stikhotvoreniia, stati, ocherki, dokladnye zapiski* (Moscow, 1956), p. 168. All translations are mine. All references to *Voynarovsky* will be to the 1956 edition, pp. 167–207.

[2] Excerpts from *Voynarovsky* were published in *Poliarnaia zvezda* between December 1823 and January 1824; *Syn otechestva*, January 19, 1824; *Sorevnovatel' prosveshcheniia i blagotvoreniia*, no. 3, 1824.

some reason Ryleev dropped these plans for the tragedy. His view of
Mazeppa at this time was not particularly unusual in the light of the official view. In the *dramatis personae* Mazeppa is described as: "Hetman of
Little Russia. A seventy-year-old man. A sly and ambitious man; a great
hypocrite, concealing his evil nature under wishful good nature towards
his country." [3] Further on, in a sketch of Mazeppa's character, he says,
"For Mazeppa, it seems, nothing was sacred, except his goal, toward
which he reached. Neither the respect rendered him by Peter, nor the
very benevolence poured on him by this great monarch, nothing could
turn him from treason. He showed cleverness in the highest degree. He
was clever about other people's fortunes, too, and found ways to claim
them." [4] This is a profound condemnation of the Hetman and a harsh
rendering of his character, but within two years Ryleev would make
Mazeppa his new hero. How and why did such a change come about?

In the preface to his *Dumy*, Ryleev quotes directly from Niemcewicz's
introduction to the *Historical Songs*, which he read in Polish, reiterating
for the Russian public the ideal use of history in literature to create in
them, especially the young, a sense of national consciousness. Though
Ryleev wrote about the Ukraine and its major historical figures—Palia,
Samoilovich, Kochubey, and Khmelnytsky—figures from the reign of
Peter I, he was also criticizing Russia's policy toward the Ukrainians.

It seems that sometime about 1823, Ryleev began to conceive of Peter
I as a tyrannical ruler. Ryleev's reading and talking about the Ukraine
probably brought this to light. About that time he began to learn the
Polish view of the Czar and of Russia. Ryleev read Polish, spoke it with
Adam Mickiewicz and that dubious Polish Russophile, Faddei Bulgarin,
and even translated some poems of Stanislaw Trębecki, a turn-of-the-
century Polish poet who often wrote on Ukrainian themes. In 1823,
Ryleev met Mickiewicz and his Polish friends, who, having been exiled
from Poland by Czar Alexander I, harbored a deep hatred for Czardom
and dreamed of an independent Poland. Mickiewicz was working on
Parts II and IV of *Forefather's Eve*, *Grażyna*, and was already contemplat-
ing *Konrad Wallenrod*. His deep hatred of Peter I and his reasons for it
were no doubt conveyed to Ryleev, whose revolutionary, patriotic zeal
grew as he became more deeply involved in loosely literary-political

---

[3] Ryleev, p. 342.   [4] *Ibid.*, pp. 342–43.

societies and with so many of the people who paved the way for the December Revolt.

In the *duma* "Peter the Great in Ostrogishka," written in 1823, Mazeppa's character is well under way to being restored in the poet's mind: "The foreigner from a barren land/ Was Mazeppa, the grey leader./ Perhaps he was still innocent,/ Perhaps he was still a hero." [5] In an unpublished fragment of the *duma* "Kochubey," also written in 1823, Ryleev clearly calls Kochubey the traitor and implies that Mazeppa was not.

> And who sold her?
> Who was the enemy of his country?
> Perhaps the best people were.
> That miserable old man Kochubey—
> A judge and a disgraceful leader.

By this time he was already writing *Voynarovsky*. [6]

It seems that Ryleev's original idea was a long poem entitled *Mazeppa*, two large fragments of which, "Gaidamak" and "Palia," are extant. Mazeppa does not appear in the 200-odd lines, but allusion is made to him. Of course, Ryleev could not have written a poem glorifying Mazeppa over Peter I, so he seems in these fragments to be toying with Scott's technique of keeping the major historical figure in the wings, while his story is told by minor characters. In this way the censors could be circumvented.

Copies of the whole manuscript of *Voynarovsky* began to circulate in Russia proper, where, for instance, Pushkin first saw it, and it went into the Ukraine and reached revolutionary circles as far as Kiev and Bessarabia. The poem was not published until February or March 1825, after it had been altered by the censors and certain footnotes had been added.

The poem is set in a plethora of historical documentation, much as Niemcewicz's *Historical Songs*. The title refers to Andrey Voynarovsky, Ivan Mazeppa's nephew, who was captured some years after Mazeppa's death at Bender and was exiled to Siberia. Originally, Ryleev was going to call the poem *The Exile*, but that title probably would not have passed the censor. A very long biographical note on Voynarovsky written by

<hr>

[5] Ryleev, p. 137.   [6] *Ibid.*, p. 373.

Bestuzhev is included in the edition as well as a long piece about Mazeppa by Alexander Kornilovich, another fellow Decembrist. Both accounts strive to present an objective historical picture. In addition to those notes, there are 18 other footnotes, presumably written by Ryleev, although the text indicates 34 footnotes. No explanation is given for the missing 16 footnotes.

The introductory poem to Bestuzhev leads one to believe that Ryleev is assuming a Byronic pose. "A lone and sad pilgrim,/ Lost on the Arabian steppes/ Full of disappointment and yearning,/ I wandered orphaned." These lines contain echoes of *Childe Harold* and the Oriental Tales: "I am cold to people;/ My soul is clouded./ Close friendships have no meaning to me." Then he shifts abruptly to: "But I saw *you*—you gave me hope." That hope is revolutionary-patriotic: "I am a citizen, not a poet." Much of Byron and *byronisme* lurks behind these lines, and Byron's death in 1824, perhaps still fresh in Ryleev's mind, prompted these remarks in this poem. In his poem on Byron's death, Ryleev says that the poet lived "for England and the world," was a "wonder of the age," and was of a mind like Socrates', a soul like Cato's, a comrade of Shakespeare.[7] It is almost in this same light that Ryleev sees himself at the opening of *Voynarovsky*. Ryleev, however, is using Byron's Oriental Tales, with their loose lines, verse paragraphs of different lengths, lines that trail off into ellipses, and almost every stock Byronic subject from the landscape to the hero as a screen for the real subject of his poem: Mazeppa and the revolutionary hero. He, like many Slavs, saw revolution in Byron's poetry and life, especially after the English Lord undertook to fight in the Greek Revolution.

Voynarovsky opens with a narrator describing the gloomy, wild, desolate Siberian landscape and moves swiftly into present events. He points out a man, left unnamed, and questions who he might be. The man is dressed like a Cossack of the Dnieper with a look like that of Byron's Conrad or Selim: restless gloom, angry forehead, clouds of yearning, deeply affecting thought. He seems to have had hard times and to be struggling with fate. When he speaks, his voice gives way to reveal his suffering.

---

[7] *Ibid.*, p. 59.

Oh my country! Oh my fields.
I shall not see you anymore;
You, graves of sacred ancestors,
The exile does not take in his arms.

Heat in vain blazes ardently;
I can not be useful.
Amid far and infamous exile,
My sentence is to languish in pain.

(I, 69–76)

To be truly Byronic, such anguish should concern a lost love and not a country. The Ukraine is not named, but his readers—if not from their knowledge of history then from the notes to the poem—would understand the inferences. As if to cover this man's first outburst of patriotism, the narrator repeats the description of the gloomy Byronic hero, obscuring a little the political impact of the speech. The first 108 lines idealize this strange exile.

Ryleev now introduces Gerhard Frederick Miller, a German who actually spent ten years roaming Russia doing a geographical survey for the Czar. Miller's character is virtually undeveloped; he acts as a kind of confessor who can hear Voynarovsky's story so that the readers may in turn hear it. Miller is lost and stumbles upon Voynarovsky, who has just shot a reindeer. After stumbling upon one another and speaking for a few moments, Voynarovsky takes the surveyor to his hovel. At line 240 the narrator changes to the first person, and Voynarovsky asks Miller if he wants to know who he is. Miller consents and is told:

—I am a miracle before you,
And a friend and relation of Mazeppa!
I am Voynarovsky.

(I 259–61)

His first form of identification is not in relation to himself but to Mazeppa, a crucial point in understanding how to read the poem. Miller is suddenly dropped until the end of the poem, the balance of which consists of Voynarovsky talking about himself and Mazeppa. It is fairly clear that on the basis of the introductory poem and the description of Voynarovsky, Ryleev identifies with Voynarovsky, who is merely the medium for Mazeppa's story; that is, Voynarovsky's political and patriotic ideas are analogous to Mazeppa's. In lines 260–77 Voynarovsky speaks about himself, again covering the implication of what he says as in the earlier lines; for every wave of patriotic feeling there is a wave of subjective and almost sentimental anguish.

At this point in the text there are editorial problems, for censor's notes are added and some lines are deleted; sometimes the latter are not designated, at other times dashes indicate omissions. The first example of such emendation occurs in the following four lines:

> Sorrow pierces my heart today;
> I am thrown upon strange fields of snow.
> Instead of mercy, let the enemy
> Show me the road to my country and my home.
>
> (I, 282–85)

The second line (line 283 in the Russian) has the following note added by the censor: "In this way Voynarovsky apologizes for the just and merciful punishment for his crime." Readers sympathetic to Peter I would understand how unrepentant and villainous Mazeppa was; Ukrainian sympathizers might smile ironically. Dashes were inserted in place of line 286: "What good are your pointless prayers!" The implication of this line in conjunction with the preceding four lines was too great to pass the censor, for the enemy is undoubtedly Russia. The censor's footnote states bluntly that Voynarovsky's punishment was justified.

The next section of this part of the poem (I, 340–450) is a domestic idyll about Voynarovsky and a young Cossack girl, who will return later in Part II as a heroine of sorts. Here Ryleev is quite obviously taking the love theme and the death-in-life experience of Byron's Mazeppa and reshaping them to apply to Voynarovsky's life. The episode with the Cossack girl is too close to be a coincidence, as a summary of it should make clear. One day the Cossacks were chasing some young Poles across the steppes—the pursuit is described as a wild ride—and they in turn are being chased by Crimean Tartars. Voynarovsky's horse dies under him and he lies injured near a burial mound. He describes his blood, sweat, and cries for help that are answered only by silence. As some ravens are about to attack him, a young Cossack girl comes to save him. She is described in detail because she becomes Voynarovsky's wife and an example of what the wife of a revolutionary should be like. The love theme, so important to Byron, is turned into a marriage theme by Ryleev. He clearly is not so interested in Byron's Theresa as he is in the

young girl who ministers to the reviving Mazeppa. If, however, Byron's
Theresa inspired Ryleev in any way, then he has transformed the Palatine's wife into a saint; in addition, unlike Byron's, Ryleev's romance ends
in married bliss that is undisturbed for three years, at which point Mazeppa is introduced into their lives.

Voynarovsky says Mazeppa was attracted to them because he loved
their children and was in turn kind to them, acting as a benevolent old
grandfather. Mazeppa brings Voynarovsky and his family to Baturyn
and the domestic-idyll theme begins to shift to Mazeppa himself. He
seems in some way troubled and a "cloud covered his face." No one
knew what the Hetman had on his mind.

> Mazeppa, secretive, as usual,
> In silence, gathered his men.
>
> (I, 471–72)

Mazeppa calls Voynarovsky to his palace to tell him a secret, but once he
knows it, Voynarovsky must give his life for the Ukraine if necessary.
Voynarovsky answers: "For my country I shall give up wife, children,
and myself—only by honor do I stand." Mazeppa answers: "I knew you
were a son of the Ukraine—a citizen. You are like me—you have a warm
heart." These lines identify Mazeppa, Voynarovsky, and Ryleev with
one another, and are almost the same words and sentiments expressed by
Ryleev in his introductory poem. Mazeppa explains himself by saying
that he is not what he seems.

> Revenge burns me—I do not stand on honor—
> I'll take off the chains, even though I violate
>   honor.
>
> (I, 510–12)

These lines give some idea of what has been called the patriotic traitor.
He sacrifices all; he cheats, lies, deceives—even kills—for the ultimate
goal: the freedom from political oppression and the establishment or re-
establishment of an independent nation. The patriotic traitor's life takes
the form of a secular martyrdom in which his sacrifice is frequently
shrouded in mystery and may be known only by some chosen few.
Mazeppa states that he respects Peter I, but will be his enemy from now
on, for his personal honor must always give way to national honor.

Voynarovsky says honor is all that matters to him, but he does not say if he means Mazeppa's kind of honor.

Mazeppa knows the outcome of his enterprise—"Either glory or eternal horror awaits me" (I, 520)—but he is willing to take the risk. The censor's note to that line is: "Such fame should have illuminated Mazeppa had he defeated Peter at the memorable Battle of Poltava; however, fame eluded him for being a traitor to Peter." Ryleev's case for Mazeppa is much too strong in these annotated lines and had to be subdued, so the censor simply dropped line 524, in which Mazeppa says that he is involved in a "struggle of freedom with despotism."

Mazeppa has now become the center of the poem. His guise is cast aside, his patriotic treason is explained, and Ryleev has made at least one point about how the revolutionaries must proceed. The emphasis shifts immediately after this outburst to the passionate musings of Voynarovsky about his misfortunes, which seems to be Ryleev's method of toning down the central theme should it become too obviously didactic. Embedded in all the Romantic feeling, longing, reflection, and description are Mazeppa's clear statements about his political position. His remarks and actions might be called a revolutionary plan of action: work in secret until the moment of the revolution. Trust only the best men. Test them adequately. Once committed to the revolution, die for it if you must.

At this point Part II begins, though there seems to be no structural or thematic reason for the break; the narrative continues uninterrupted. Light is dawning outside as Miller and Voynarovsky continue. Voynarovsky comments that he was always happy when he was fighting. As he tells it, Poltava was doomed to be a defeat from the start. Charles XII is wounded and flees with Mazeppa, Voynarovsky, and their entourage. They stop one night and Mazeppa's soliloquy is recounted. This situation is also like that in Byron's *Mazeppa* and the sense of what he says is close to what Mazeppa says there. These lines, however, were altered.

Original, uncensored version

O, how wrong we are to find the world blessed!
O, how dependent we are upon fate!
There, in the soul, boils audacity.
Terror came with the struggle.

In one instant all was resolved.
In one instant all was lost,
Forever my native country's
Hope, happiness, and peace.
Was Mazeppa humiliated by it?
What did I gain?

Censored, Published version

O, how wrong we are to find the world blessed!
O, how dependent we are upon fate!
There, in the soul, boils audacity.
The world struggle comes to an end.
In one instant all was resolved.
In one instant all was lost.
Was Mazeppa humiliated by it?
What did I gain?

(II, 649–58)

Mazeppa concludes that he and Peter lived for the same ends: the nation and fame in war. Are they both right? Both great? There is no direct answer in the poem. A soldier from Baturyn enters and tells Mazeppa that Peter is banqueting in the Hetman's palace, adding

You, Mazeppa, like Judas,
The Ukrainians curse everywhere.

Mazeppa's lands have been confiscated and his name has been effaced from all public buildings. He is overcome, for his prophecy has come true; fame has eluded him and he will become a traitor in the people's minds. In Byron's poem, the Hetman even after his defeat is still hopeful about the future, but Ryleev's hero despairs. The point here is surely that Mazeppa will be misunderstood and misinterpreted in the history books of the future.

Voynarovsky then says that he does not know what Mazeppa's motives were:

We saw in him the chief of the nation.
We considered him a father.
We saw in him our homeland.
I do not know if he wanted
To save the Ukrainian nation from trouble

Or to set in her a throne for himself—
To me the Hetman did not divulge his secret.

(II, 698–704)

Later, Voynarovsky calls him "sly" (II, 705), and still later he says, "I would be the first to strike him down,/ If I knew he was an enemy of the people" (II, 715–16). But Voynarovsky did not. In Part I, Mazeppa has told Voynarovsky his secret plan. Are there deeper secrets? The doubts that Voynarovsky expresses are those planted by Peter and his men. Voynarovsky questions: if I do not know this, how could anyone else? He again launches into a hymn to the Ukraine and his love for it in order to blur the point—so strongly but subtly made—that Mazeppa was in the right.

Next he recounts Mazeppa's death, which he and Orlik, Mazeppa's successor, have witnessed. He suffers for twelve days, hallucinating about Kochubey and Iskra, Peter's anger, Kochubey's wife and daughter, yet always wanting to hide his pain from his people. The last words he utters are "Peter, Motherland." Peter thought Mazeppa was his good friend, but according to this poem, Mazeppa did not actually reciprocate those feelings. These words, so juxtaposed, would pacify the censor and give the czarist readers a sense that Mazeppa knew at the end that he had erred; but the revolutionaries would know that "motherland" was the only word that mattered. The ambiguity is deliberate. Voynarovsky's last comments about Mazeppa were garbled by the censor. The actual lines are: "O stranger, we all buried/ Our country's freedom with Mazeppa," which meant that since Mazeppa's time there had been no one to fight for Ukrainian independence. These lines were changed to read: "O, stranger, stranger, all dreamed/ Who with Mazeppa buried/ The hope of our country," giving the impression that people who put their hopes in Mazeppa were unrealistic and naive about the Hetman.

The poem's last section traces Voynarovsky's wandering after Mazeppa's death. Ryleev makes a parallel between the turmoil of Voynarovsky's soul and the turmoil in nature. Byron also used this device. Voynarovsky is exiled to Siberia, despondent. Miraculously, his wife finds him and, as earlier, restores him to life. Voynarovsky's wife is not the mysterious, bewitching lady of Byron's tale, but "a citizen and a wife." The reader is to recall here, no doubt, Ryleev's "I am not a poet, but a citizen"; she and Voynarovsky make the perfect revolutionary couple.

Voynarovsky then muses about Brutus, although the name is left out of the 1825 edition:

> Great was Brutus, who defended Rome.
> He had greatness in his deeds, and freedom in his heart,
> But posterity did not give him the laurel crown,
> No example will renew him.
> He lost his citizenship [originally, "He lost his freedom."]
> For by suicide he gave triumph to his enemies.
>
> (II, 1003–10)

This is Ryleev's final estimate of Mazeppa and it certainly could not pass the censor. Brutus's suicidal attempt to save Rome by killing Caesar is analogous to Mazeppa's treason against Peter. Brutus's noble gesture obscured his name because he lost, so too with Mazeppa. Both were patriotic traitors.

The following lines were deleted from *Voynarovsky;* an ellipsis indicated such. They contain a call for the emergence of a revolutionary leader.

> It still may be that a comrade of the people will arise
> And will save the unfortunate countrymen,
> And their land.
> Freedom will finally be resurrected.
>
> (II, 1017–20)

Such a man might still free the Ukraine, and by extension that same kind of man could lead the Russian Revolution, so evidently on Ryleev's mind at the writing of *Voynarovsky*. Unfortunately, he did not appear either for the Ukraine or for the Decembrists. One should notice Ryleev's language here, for it has messianic overtones: a comrade may arise from the people to become their savior by resurrecting their freedom.

The image of Mazeppa that emerges from *Voynarovsky*, however, is one of bold, clever, ruthless patriotism. He is much more serious than Byron's Hetman and nothing at all like the versions of Hugo or the French painters. There is something of the Napoleonic duality in him: that sense of a liberal idealist moving closer and closer to realism that turns into fanaticism. Perhaps Ryleev sensed that it would be natural for such a mind to develop a tendency toward messianism. Pushkin sees only the Napoleonic parallel in his characterization of Mazeppa in *Poltava*. Ryleev exonerates Mazeppa for his desperate and secretive tactics; because the time and the leaders of the opposition were also more tyrannous and despotic, rather desperate remedies were needed to cure desperate ills. For Ryleev, the contemporary political situation was equally desperate.

A great deal has been made of *Voynarovsky* critically and politically since Lenin called the December Revolt Russia's first step toward the Proletarian Revolution. As Bohdan Galster points out, Ryleev and the poets in his camp saw literature as a legitimate forum in which to argue for the rebuilding of the government and society.[8] He used the usual Romantic techniques, so pleasing to the nineteenth-century readers (gloomy landscapes, mysteriously depressed protagonist, the detail of history and fact, which he converts by the end of the poem) as camouflage for his theme: the revolutionary hero and the general scheme for carrying out the revolution.

Voynarovsky is an answer to a special reading of Byron's *Mazeppa*. What was appealing to Ryleev about Byron's Mazeppa was that character's sense of revolt for the good of the Ukrainian people; Byron and his Mazeppa were thus interpreted as examples of political protest. It should be obvious that *Voynarovsky* was a dangerous poem in the year that it was published, and that *Mazeppa* could be too, depending upon who was interpreting it.

When the revolt broke out in December 1825, and Ryleev, Bestuzhev, Kornilovich, Rayevsky, and Somorov were implicated, the poem was considered practically treasonous, and those associated with it came under suspicion. In many ways Ryleev fell into the trap that his hero Mazeppa had; the revolution was exposed at the wrong time and defeat was inevitable.

Using the same basic sources as Ryleev, Pushkin makes *Poltava* his answer to *Voynarovsky*. He was much more interested in Peter than he was in Mazeppa, for his family was connected to the Czar's in the seventeenth and eighteenth centuries, and in poems, tales, a partially finished novel, and in history, he occupied himself with Peter and the time of

---

[8] Bohdan Galster, "Powieść poetycka Rylejewa," *Slavia Orientalis* 10 (Warsaw, 1961): 17–18.

his reign. Mazeppa was at first merely a footnote to that interest, but one that seemed to lengthen and involve odd cross-references. Pushkin's interest in the Hetman dates from at least 1824, when he and I. P. Liprandi, a young officer he met in Kishinev who became a close friend, made a short trip to Teraspol and Bender to interview a man reputed to be 136 years old who was supposed to have taken part in the campaign of Peter against Charles XII. The second object of the trip was to find the grave of Mazeppa at Bender.[9]

In that same year, Pushkin read Ryleev's *Voynarovsky*, which he admired very much and which very probably was his major inspiration to write *Poltava*. The first written comments about *Voynarovsky* are laudatory. "For *Voynarovsky*. Our literature has been needing this poem." [10] Something about the poem caught his interest but nowhere does he spell it out. Jokingly, at one point, he remarks to his brother that he hopes Ryleev will put "our grandfather [his maternal great-grandfather Hannibal] in Peter's suite." [11] In a letter to his friend Prince Vyazemsky he says that Ivan Kozlov's *Black Monk* is "more intelligent" than *Voynarovsky*, but that in Ryleev's poem there is more "abandon or dash" in the style.[12] These initial reactions seem either amusingly personal or concerned with style. Though the letter does not survive, there is reference to it in another that shows Pushkin must have sent Ryleev a detailed, extremely favorable, criticism of the poem.[13]

At this time Pushkin does not seem at all interested in the political implications of *Voynarovsky*, but then he was already in exile in Mikhaylovskoe for his rebellious and atheistic tendencies. What he did not need was political intrigue. It must have been a difficult time for him, for many of his friends who were much more active in subversive political activity had no strictures imposed upon them. After the December Revolt, references to *Voynarovsky* disappear from his correspondence. In his notes in preparation for his article answering the critics of *Poltava*, he tells how important Ryleev's poem was to the creation of *Poltava* and clearly shows his attitude toward the Hetman.

---

[9] Ernest J. Simmons, *Pushkin* (Cambridge, Mass.: Harvard University Press, 1937), p. 166.

[10] J. Thomas Shaw, ed. & tr., *The Letters of Alexander Pushkin*, 3 vols. (Bloomington: Indiana University Press, 1963) 1:147.

[11] *Ibid.*, p. 278.   [12] *Ibid.*, p. 226.   [13] *Ibid.*, p. 220.

When I read for the first time in *Voynarovsky* these lines:

> He sees Kochubey's unhappy wife
> And her poor daughter. How shameless. . . .

I was surprised how it was that the poet did not restrain himself in such dramatic circumstances. . . . How repulsive that is! Not one sincere, good feeling, not one pleasing trait! Seduction, hatred, treason, hypocrisy, cowardice, and cruelty. Strong traits and deep, tragic shadow covering that awfulness—that intrigued me.[14]

Pushkin's attitude toward *Voynarovsky* seems to have changed over the years. His enthusiasm shifted to direct opposition, and *Poltava* turns out to be a statement of Pushkin's proimperial views.

Most of his life Pushkin publicly demonstrated his loyalty to the Czar and to the aristocracy. Some like to point to his ode "André Chenier," written in 1825, as his statement of sentiment for the Decembrists.[15] As the poem's subject is a French poet who was executed by the Jacobins, one might associate it with the Decembrists by indirection; but Pushkin was primarily interested in the stylistic aspects of Chenier's poetry, and in addition he conceived of Chenier's imprisonment as an analogue for his own exile in the country. Pushkin's friends and the public may have thought the poem had wider implications, but he did not. Because of the exile imposed on him by the government, Pushkin was interested in the interference by any government with the lives of individuals, especially poets. Some of his close friends were freethinking liberals, and one gets the impression that he flirted with these ideas to please them and not out of any deep political convictions. He was consistently, though to varying intensities, an aristocrat and a royalist throughout his life.

The December Revolt failed; Pushkin in Mikhailovskoe did not know about the fate of his friends, and pondered his own. It has often been said that had he been in St. Petersburg he would have participated in the Revolt,[16] but he was never associated with the secret societies, never knew any of their plans, does not seem to have been interested in the Revolt, and when he did learn the details he wanted to clear himself. In January 1826, he wrote to Vasyl Zhukhovsky giving proof of his "new

---

[14] *Pushkin: Polnoe sobranie sochinenii* (Moscow, 1949), 11:160.

[15] G. M. Lenobl', *Istoriia i literatura* (Moscow, 1960), p. 319.

[16] D. S. Mirsky, *Pushkin* (New York: Dutton, 1963), pp. 93–94.

virtue" in an attempt to convince the new Czar, Nicholas I, to end his exile.[17]

Nicholas I's new secret police under Count Benckendorff sent an agent to Mikhailovskoe to investigate Pushkin's activities. He was cleared of any suspicion and was summoned to appear before the Czar in August. What transpired at that interview is not known, but probably Pushkin swore his faith to the Czar and the Czar decided to become Pushkin's personal censor. As it turned out, this was not a favor, for from that point on Pushkin was watched by the secret police and every word he wrote had to pass Count Benckendorff. Pushkin seemed to be proving his loyalty all the time now, and always he felt under suspicion. The Czar simply did not trust very many writers. The one exception seems to have been Faddei Bulgarin, who had the right to publish the only official daily paper in St. Petersburg; but that strange man's relations with the rest of the Russian literary establishment, including Pushkin, were increasingly unpleasant to the point of hatred. After Pushkin's reconciliation with the Czar, his work became generally oriented toward Russian nationalism and the evocation of Russian life.

Pushkin's zeal for history and his literary gifts focused on the virtues of Russia and her Czars. Perhaps, as Troyat suggests, the writing of *Poltava* was prompted by a direct attack on his loyalty to the crown.[18] On October 2, 1828, Count Tolstoy interrogated Pushkin about his scatological poem *Gavriliada*, written much earlier, and about his loyalty to the Czar. The next day *Poltava* was begun and by about October 15 it was completed.[19] One cannot say assuredly that the interview with Count Tolstoy had a direct bearing upon the writing of *Poltava*, but the probability that Pushkin desired to show his loyalty seems strong.

The prose introduction, published in the first edition but not in subsequent ones, states Pushkin's political attitude. His major claim is to historical accuracy: "It would be better to unfold and bring to the light the actual characters of the seditious Hetman and not to distort willfully the historical picture." Ryleev, he says, erred in making Mazeppa a "hero of liberty," and that is Pushkin's major criticism of *Voynarovsky* in 1829. He softens this attack on Ryleev by criticizing Egor Aladin (a

[17] Shaw, *Letters*, 1:302–3.
[18] Henri Troyat, *Pouchkine: Biographie* (Paris, 1953), pp. 445–46.
[19] Lenobl', p. 302.

prose writer who contributed many short stories to the popular almanacs of the day), who pictured the Hetman as "an old coward, getting pale when confronting an armed woman." He adds that Charles XII made the same mistake that Napoleon did by thinking that he could overwhelm Russia's strength.[20] Pushkin, like Byron, sees the similarity between the defeats of Charles and Napoleon, and this introduction is the first indication that Pushkin has *Mazeppa* in mind as well as *Voynarovsky*. The political view places Pushkin squarely in the Czar's camp.

As I have noted, Pushkin had been interested in Mazeppa and related themes for some time. In addition to his trip to Bender and his interest in Ryleev's poem, by 1827 he was working on his novel, *The Nigger of Peter the Great*, which deals with Mazeppa's time. Not to be underestimated, however, was Pushkin's association with Adam Mickiewicz, whom he was seeing quite a lot of in 1828. They discussed Peter I, Mazeppa, and probably Ryleev, whom Mickiewicz admired. All three bear upon *Poltava*. How much these discussions with Mickiewicz weighed upon Pushkin's mind is difficult to determine, but surely Pushkin was affected by the Pole's hatred of czardom and his zeal for revolutionary independence movements. From what is known of these talks, it seems that Pushkin continually argued that history repudiated Mickiewicz's claims.[21] With regard to Mazeppa, history clearly showed Pushkin that the Hetman was a traitor to Russia and to the Ukrainians. *Poltava* seems to be his final view of the matter. Pushkin sent Mickiewicz a published copy of *Poltava*, and Mickiewicz sent in return a copy of Byron's poetry. In a couple of years Pushkin would turn against Poland, and Mickiewicz would bid his farewell in a short poem, "To My Muscovite Friends." The Polish insurrection of 1830 was a demonstration of anti-Russian feeling that Pushkin could not tolerate and in which Mickiewicz exulted.[22] Most likely all of Pushkin's associations with the Mazeppa theme came to focus in that interview with Count Tolstoy, and *Poltava* took shape in his mind on that unpleasant day in October 1828.

To argue for one or more particular influences seems futile, for Push-

[20] Alexander Pushkin, *Sobranie sochinenii* (Moscow, 1960), 3:449–50. I have been unable to locate E. Aladin's *Kochubey*. It was published in 1827 and is, I think, a short story.

[21] Lenobl', p. 325.

[22] Wacław Lednicki, *Pouchkine et la Pologne: à propos de la trilogie antipolonaise de Pouchkine* (Paris, 1928), p. 12.

kin's notes to *Poltava* indicate that he used Bantysh-Kamensky's *History of the Ukraine*, Voltaire's *History of Charles XII* and *The History of Russia under the Reign of Peter the Great*, Peter I's *Journal*, and Byron's *Mazeppa*. He probably also used the *History of the People of Rus'* in manuscript and the works of Feofan Prokopovich, Bishop of Novogorod under Peter I. He corresponded with Bantysh-Kamensky, who probably knew more about Mazeppa than anyone alive at that time. The poem is steeped in historical fact, seemingly in accord with what he set out to do in the introduction. It is useful to recall that Pushkin not only used history in literature but also spent a considerable part of his life in studying and writing about history in a scholarly way.

As one reads the poem, one feels that Pushkin was really obsessed with his purpose, for the historical material is inserted in large chunks in a tone that is different from the rest of the poem. It is not a grand synthesis of historical material, however, as all of his characters are highly fictionalized creations. And as for the sequence of events, he takes the story of Mazeppa's affair with his goddaughter, Maria Kochubey, and Mazeppa's disagreement with her father and telescopes them to make all of these events immediately precede the Battle of Poltava in 1708, although they actually took place in 1704–5. As for the characters, he takes the bold outlines of their personalities, much as Bertuch did, and fills in psychological details, creates confrontations, and interprets their motives—not all of which can be deduced from the historical material even today. Peter I, for instance, supposedly the hero of the poem, appears briefly in the third canto; he is seen only from a distance. No time is spent defining his character; his greatness is assumed and merely pronounced in the poem. It is difficult to say whether Pushkin is using Scott's technique of keeping the major figure in the background, or whether he is afraid to cope with the material directly for some political reason. One only knows that Peter is not the center of the poem and that what Pushkin does say about him is not so historically accurate. Pushkin's technique is to take his characters out of historical context and (as in the case of Peter, because he was the victor and czar) create what he thinks are the traits of a victorious emperor, whether or not they apply to the man's character as inferred from history. He seems to have some general concept of an emperor in mind. The same treatment is given to the traitor Mazeppa and the martyr Kochubey. The result is a curious mixture of fact and fiction that gives the reader the impression that he is being exposed to historical account. There is, of course, nothing unorthodox about such license, but Pushkin insists that he is not fictionalizing his material. It is not quite the same device that was so common in eighteenth-century novels, or for instance in Dorville's *Memoires d'Azéma,* for Pushkin says that he will argue from the facts to set historical misconception straight. He is not fictionalizing history, rather he sees himself verifying fact through his poem. When he wrote his critical defense of *Poltava,* however, he seemed to have changed his mind.

One of the problems in considering *Poltava* is its structure, for, unlike *Mazeppa* and *Voynarovsky,* it is not a continuous narrative. This has led some critics to see it as three separate poems, the last of which, the Battle of Poltava, makes the real point of the entire work. *Poltava* is hardly a narrative poem at all; it is conceived more like a three-act play with an all-purpose narrator to keep the material together. The narrator, at the opening of the poem, gives character sketches of Kochubey, Maria, and Mazeppa—much the sort of thing one often finds preceding the text of a play, and dialogues and soliloquies make up a large portion of the poem. In Canto II the narrator sets the scene for a dialogue and provides the shift to a new setting for another dialogue. Sometimes he breaks out, as in Canto II, to hymn the praises of Peter I, but the narrator is not an objective observer, as some have interpreted him,[23] for he clearly sides with Kochubey against Mazeppa and Maria from the beginning, though he does not too often comment directly upon the actions and motivations of the characters.

The narrator's apparent sympathy for Mazeppa's love for Maria has led some critics to feel that he, and by implication Pushkin, was trying to soften his attack on the Hetman, if not actually condoning his action. This, however, is a strained reading of the poem and overlooks the attitude of the author in his introductory defense of it. A great deal has also been made of the treatment of love as it reflects Pushkin's own love life at the time of writing. The dedicatory poem is addressed to a lady still not positively identified, and that sort of approach to *Poltava* seems not pertinent to the one theme that is continually stressed: Mazeppa's duplicity, which leads to his betrayal of the great Czar.

[23] John Pauls, *Pushkin's 'Poltava'* (New York: Shevchenko Scientific Society, 1962), p. 41.

Pushkin never loses sight of the political implications of the actions of his characters, yet there is some sense in his conception of Mazeppa that the man faced real moral dilemmas and unfortunately resolved them incorrectly. No matter how loving Mazeppa may appear in this poem, it is clear that he always acts treacherously. The narrator sometimes hesitates to make the final pronouncement about the Hetman's treason, which may give the impression that Pushkin himself was uncertain about his generally ruthless treatment of Mazeppa. But to read into the narrator's occasional vacillation an Aesopian interpretation that makes Mazeppa the hero of the poem is incorrect. Pushkin wanted to be fair to Mazeppa historically, to be objective, and what one sees in the odd moments in the poem are attempts to give the Hetman some redeeming features. Without them he might easily turn into a caricature. Pushkin, however, drew back each time, probably for fear that he would be misinterpreted, that readers, and the Czar, might construe the heroism of Mazeppa. Ultimately, he stacked the cards against the Hetman, feeling, perhaps, that he had to make his political position on this important historical issue very clear.[24]

The first glimpse of Mazeppa is given in Canto I by the narrator.

> He is old. He is weighed down by age,
> Wars, cares, troubles;
> But feelings boil in him, and once again
> Mazeppa knows love.
>
> (I, 41–44)[25]

This is followed by an analysis of how love affects the old man, of how his feelings change every day because of Maria Kochubey. When Kochubey's wife learns of them, she lashes out at her daughter, calling Mazeppa "shameless" and a "madman." Maria faints, feigns illness, and mysteriously disappears from home on the second night. The narrator then turns his attention to Kochubey and his wife, and spends a good deal of time trying to make Kochubey into a tragic figure. While so doing, the narrator exposes his bias:

[24] Pushkin surely knew about Mickiewicz's *Konrad Wallenrod* at this time and how that poem was supposed to be read, but there is no reason to believe that he wanted *Poltava* to be read in the same way. M. Aronson, " 'Konradvallenrod' i 'Poltava,' " *Vremenik Pushkinde Komissii* 2 (1936): 53.

[25] All citations are my translation from Alexander Pushkin, *Sochinenia* (Moscow, 1960), 3:192–239.

And soon Kochubey hears
The fatal piece of news:
She [Maria] has murdered shame and honor.
She is in the arms of a robber!
Such disgrace! The father and mother,
It is said, forgot how to smile.

(I, 99–104)

And one wonders whether Pushkin may have had in mind Ryleev's
duma "Kochubey," where the opposite view of Mazeppa's old friend is
held. Ryleev's disgraceful old Kochubey seems ennobled by Pushkin at
the expense of Mazeppa's reputation. Kochubey was furious with Mazeppa for taking Maria, but, he recalls, Mazeppa had been his good
friend, which in turn adds to his anger. He conceives what he thinks is a
devastating revenge: to expose Mazeppa's treachery to Peter I.

What follows is a short history of the political situation involving Russia, the Ukraine, and Sweden. The tone shifts and the language is rather
like a versification of history, rather like what Muśnicki did in his "epic"
Pułtawa. While the youth of the Ukraine are clamoring for war, Mazeppa
seemingly rules calmly, paying no attention to their verbal attacks on
him, in which they brand him a burned-out old man, no longer able to
lead. They recall the old heroes who fought against the hated Muscovites, all of whom had the power of the army behind them, which Mazeppa did not. One recalls that Mazeppa himself in his poems lamented
the scattering of Ukrainian youth among the Poles, Russians, and Turks;
Pushkin may have known of this and wanted to show to the contrary
that the young people had no faith in their Hetman. The narrator goes
out of his way to extol the virtues of Bohdan Khmelnytsky, much as the
young Ryleev did, but Pushkin undoubtedly has in mind the political
compromises Khmelnytsky made with the Russians. This section of the
poem seems almost a parody of sections of *Voynarovsky*. Voynarovsky
asks a series of rhetorical questions about Mazeppa's motives, and Pushkin's narrator does too, but he reaches definite conclusions where Voynarovsky did not.

Who can read the mind,
Penetrate the fatal abyss
Of insidious souls? Souls in which
The fruit of depressed horror
Lies deeply hidden,
And the plans of the past,

Perhaps, ripen slowly?
How does one know? That is why Mazeppa is angry,
Why his heart is sly and false,
That is why he is not careful
And why his manner seems so casual.

(I, 205–10)

Voynarovsky does not speculate about these dark motives. The nature of these old plans is not disclosed at this point, and the narrator, in the form of a litany, lists Mazeppa's faults. Pushkin's castigation of Mazeppa follows closely the probable source of this indictment: Peter I's universals addressed to the Ukrainian people in 1708–9.[26] Pushkin seems most interested in demonstrating how these bad qualities bear upon Mazeppa's various personal betrayals; first he deals with the betrayal of Kochubey, then with Peter I.

Kochubey decides to inform the Czar about Mazeppa's plans, for the Hetman had confided his plans for freeing the Ukraine to his old friend in their intimate conversations. Pushkin does not seem bothered that Kochubey is also betraying his friend and for petty reasons. If Mazeppa's plan means the salvation of the Ukraine, is not Kochubey's betrayal more sinister than Mazeppa's? One might think so, but Pushkin, who considered the Ukraine a part of Russia and not an independent nation, probably did not.

More and more evidence is presented against Mazeppa. The Polish Jesuit Zaleński, messenger of Princess Dolska, is introduced; through the Princess Mazeppa is dealing with the Polish government. According to Pushkin, if Mazeppa joined the Poles against the Russians, he would be given the Ukrainian throne. On all sides the Hetman seems to be intriguing against Peter. Unexpectedly, a message from the Czar arrives assuring him that his loyalty is unquestioned, and this is the first Mazeppa learns of the defection of Kochubey and Iskra. Mazeppa reasons that Kochubey should not have become involved in this intrigue, which will bring about his own downfall. As for Maria, she made the choice to leave her parents herself and Mazeppa does not feel responsible for her or what may happen to her. Pushkin illustrates Mazeppa's ruthlessness by having him sacrifice even the girl he loves to achieve his goal. Ry-

---

[26] Pauls, p. 47. Pauls says that the negative description is a verified paraphrase of Feofan Prokopovich, pp. 26–27.

leev's Mazeppa also says that he must sacrifice all honor to win his nation's independence—for Ryleev saw that as a necessary trait of the revolutionary leader—but his Hetman seems less calloused. Obviously, Pushkin could not tolerate a man who sinned against the aristocratic virtue of honor, and focused upon Mazeppa's betrayal of those close to him in order to show the depth of the Hetman's treachery.

The second canto is composed of five dramatic scenes: a dialogue between Mazeppa and Maria, a description that leads to a dialogue between Kochubey and Orlik that in turn becomes a soliloquy by Mazeppa, a conversation between Maria and her mother, and a description of the execution of Kochubey and Iskra and the subsequent disappearance of Maria. In the conversation with Maria, Mazeppa appears preoccupied and Maria thinks he is bored with her. He explains that his mood has nothing to do with her but with his old plans:

> For a long time we have been planning;
> Now it brews among us.
> It has ripened over a time;
> A great struggle is ahead of us.
> Without sweet freedom and glory
> We buried our heads for a long time
> Under the protection of Warsaw,
> Under the power of Moscow.
> But the independent power.
> Of the Ukraine will be a terrible time:
> The bloody banner of freedom
> I shall lift over Peter.

(II, 58–69)

Maria is delighted to learn that if he succeeds, the throne of the Ukraine will be his. Whereas Voynarovsky was a confidant of and party to this plan in Ryleev's poem, Pushkin uses it to pacify a woman's jealousy; Maria already sees herself as a great queen, and she volunteers to do anything for Mazeppa. She does not yet know that her father is to be executed, so she does not realize she is being duped into choosing between her father and Mazeppa. Her eagerness to join Mazeppa salves his conscience about her father's execution and encourages him to carry out his other plans. The word that Pushkin continually uses to describe Mazeppa is *khitry*, which means self-seeking cleverness. It is by far the dominant characteristic of the Hetman as Pushkin envisioned him and is especially applicable to this scene. Pushkin, one is reminded, was inspired in part to write *Poltava* when he read those two lines in *Voynarovsky* about Maria and her mother, and in this scene that inspiration is realized.

Now that Mazeppa's plans are in execution, nothing must stand in their way, and Pushkin begins to explore Mazeppa's megalomania in detail. Mazeppa contemplates his friendship with Kochubey, prompted by a shout he hears, which takes on more and more sinister overtones as Mazeppa thinks about it. Dawn comes and he walks about the garden, troubled about what he must do but determined to do it.

The scene shifts to Maria's room, where her mother comes to ask her to beg Mazeppa for Kochubey's life. Maria is astounded by the news of her father's impending execution and faints, and with almost cinematic rapidity of transition the execution is described in brutal detail. The crowd watches awestruck, but afterward they disperse casually and go on with their daily work. Two women appear—undoubtedly Maria and her mother, though they are not named—only to learn that Kochubey has already been executed. The scene fades to Mazeppa, who is moving away from the place of execution, not saying a word. He returns home and looks for Maria, but she is gone. He sends out a search party, but no one can find her and the canto ends:

> The trace of her existence
> Disappeared like a sound in the desert,
> And her mother in obscure banishment
> Dashed away her grief in poverty.
>
> (II, 509–12)

Her disappearance is not explained. It was one of Pushkin's favorite techniques to leave loose ends in his plot to create a sense of mystery. Maria's disappearance recalls Theresa's in *Mazeppa*, but Pushkin does not tell his readers Mazeppa's reaction.

On the basis of these two cantos alone it is difficult to say categorically that Mazeppa is the central character of the poem. He is unquestionably the villain, but he shares the stage with Kochubey and Maria. Kochubey was probably conceived as the hero of the poem because he possesses that sense of honor which Pushkin considered the most noble virtue. The young Maria is at first duped by her love for the old Hetman and by the prospect of being a queen, but once Mazeppa's duplicity is exposed, she leaves him, and the promises he extracted from her do not count because they were made under false pretenses. Mazeppa is left abandoned by everyone at the end of the canto, but as yet there is no clue to his state of mind.

Canto III is far less dramatic than the others, containing instead much historical material. The reason for Mazeppa's alliance with Charles XII and why it was a deception is explained by the narrator. Mazeppa feigned a mortal illness, called priests around him, and seemed on the verge of dying—all to divert the Russians; but on the day before the battle he got out of bed, apparently healthy and an avowed enemy of Peter I. The Russians, however, discover the ploy and prepare for war. Once Peter learns of the trick, he makes amends with the families of Kochubey and Iskra, and the exiled Palia is called back to the army. The Ukrainians grumble that Mazeppa has overstepped his bounds this time, for they are not nearly so prepared to fight as they should be. Throughout, Pushkin has been showing that the Ukrainians were discontented with Mazeppa's leadership, and although there was a historical basis for such a division of feeling among the people, Pushkin slants it all negatively, giving the impression that Mazeppa carried out this plan single-handedly and without any support from his countrymen.

The day before the battle Mazeppa tells Orlik that he realizes that his plan will not work and that Charles XII cannot beat the Russians. Orlik proposes that Mazeppa try to reach an agreement with Peter, but Mazeppa says it is too late. He exposes his real motivation for his betrayal of Peter: at a feast with Peter I, after the victory of the Battle of Azov, Mazeppa spoke boldly to the Czar, who, angered by the Hetman's presumption, dropped his cup of wine and pulled Mazeppa's ear. Mazeppa was so humiliated that he decided that night to get his revenge, and he has harbored it all these years. Poltava is to be his moment of revenge. Such, it seems, had been Mazeppa's motivation from the start.

This anecdote in one form or another had been passed down since Voltaire's *Histoire* and Dorville's novel. Mazeppa was either slapped in the face or had wine thrown into it or had his beard or ears pulled. If Mazeppa did act in concert with the Swedes out of such trivial motives, then certainly his stature as a great leader is immensely undercut. The whole idea, then, of fighting for Ukrainian independence was merely a ruse for his personal outrage. Pushkin has carefully prepared the reader for this revelation by continually emphasizing Mazeppa's selfishness in all his personal relationships; yet it hardly seems plausible in the poem. Orlik does not respond to Mazeppa's explanation and disappears from the rest of the poem. In fact, no action on this new information is taken by anyone, and the scene merely shifts to the Battle itself. This estimate of Mazeppa's motivation is perhaps the most condemning view of him in this poem or in any of the works about him, for it obviates any heroic qualities that Byron or Ryleev either stated or implied about him. The critics attacked Pushkin for his interpretation of the Hetman's action, but Pushkin asserted that he was only being historically accurate.

The Battle of Poltava is described with brilliant economy. Peter enters the battlefield, rallying his men and urging them on to victory. Mazeppa watches this from the sidelines, thoughtful, and surrounded by his faithful Cossacks. He hears a shot and turns around to see Voynarovsky holding a smoking musket and a young Cossack dying nearby. The young man, who was in love with Maria and had carried the message from Kochubey to the Czar, had tried to assassinate his Hetman. Pushkin has *Voynarovsky* very much in mind here and not only because he introduces the character into the poem. Voynarovsky, talking about Brutus, suggests that perhaps the best way to save the Ukraine is to kill the Czar. Pushkin has another solution in mind: kill Mazeppa. The young man dies with Maria's name on his lips, but Mazeppa knows nothing about it and seems indifferent to the man's death. Pushkin is of course trying to shore up his plot, but is also showing that the supposedly loyal Cossacks are turning against Mazeppa.

The Battle is lost, Charles and Mazeppa flee, and Peter I holds a victory feast. As the two leaders flee across the steppes, Mazeppa sees his burned home and recalls Maria and the good times he had there; his thoughts are very much like Kochubey's meditation before his death. They camp that night and Mazeppa dreams, or thinks he dreams, that Maria comes to him. She accuses him of slyness, and reminds him of her father's execution, saying she will not forgive Mazeppa, taunting him with Kochubey's death. Mazeppa's soul seems disturbed by what he has done, but he has no sense of repentance. The dawn comes and the group moves on.

The poem ends with an epilogue. The narrator says that a hundred years have passed, and asks what is left of these brave, strong men? All has passed, including "the bloody traces of the effects, of defeat and victory." Only from time to time does some stranger come to look at Mazeppa's grave, as Pushkin had done: "Forgotten Mazeppa from the old days!" He is recalled only in the anathema in the churches each year, but the martyrs' graves, Kochubey's and Iskra's, are well preserved by the Church. As for Maria, tradition is silent about her. Her fate is hidden, and only from time to time does some blind Ukrainian singer tell the story of the sinful girl. The poem tapers off quietly, its tone subdued and nostalgic.

The epilogue seems to be an answer to *Voynarovsky*. At the end of that poem there was hope a new leader would arise to fight again; however Pushkin asserts that all such hopes have been long forgotten. What was so upsetting to Pushkin about Ryleev's point of view was that it was contrary to Russian nationalistic policy, which asserted Russia's right to rule the Slavic peoples. Any ethnic distinctions, though admitted, were to be superseded by a grand concept of Russian nationalism, and so it appeared in nineteenth-century Russian historiography. Pushkin was insisting upon that view.

But quite obviously Mazeppa had not been forgotten, as the narrator would have the reader believe, for Pushkin's poem itself brought the name before the public again. Had Pushkin set the historical facts straight? Apparently he thought so; but the public did not, for the poem was not a success, which perturbed him. In part, the readers were annoyed by the strange construction of the poem and the odd shifting from character to character. In part, too, they saw it as an attack on *Voynarovsky* and perhaps even upon the martyred poet himself. *Poltava* made Pushkin's political leanings clear: he was for the Czar and against revolution; he believed in the monarchy and was against independence movements.

As there had been twenty reviews of the poem, none favorable, Pushkin felt compelled to answer the critics in 1831. In a short and bitter article,[27] Pushkin claimed that his poem was a totally original creation, but that Mazeppa's character was historically accurate as far as he was concerned. The ear-pulling episode came from *Kosinsky's Chronicles* and was, he emphasized, an accurate interpretation of the Hetman's motivation.

[27] "*Otryvok iz rukopisi Pushkina (Poltava)*," *Dennitsa* (1831): 124–30.

He attacked Byron for being struck by the picture of the man as seen in the apocryphal story of the wild ride, yet did not seem aware that the story he used was probably equally spurious. Byron, he said, used very broad brush strokes to create a character who had no relation to the historical figure, but Pushkin's own brush strokes were equally as broad. All in all, his defense is not very convincing, and seems more the outburst of a poet whose poem did not please the public. *Poltava* was, after all, his first taste of literary failure.

The image of Mazeppa that emerges from *Poltava* is almost a caricature of a petty villain. For all his insistence upon historicity, Pushkin has slanted the facts, though as a poet he had every right to alter the material as he pleased; however, to claim otherwise was falsifying what he actually produced. *Poltava* was not the last work about Mazeppa in Eastern Europe, but it was the last to deal effectively with the East European legend of the traitor. Of course *Voynarovsky* was remembered, but Ryleev's work was suppressed after the December Revolt and did not appear again for many decades. *Poltava* saw many printings.[28]

The Mazeppa theme had almost run its course in Eastern Europe, and in these early years of Polish and Russian Romanticism, fraught with political intrigues and unrest, the Hetman had proved a convenient medium for nationalism, freedom, and revolt. There was nothing symbolic about him, no play of aesthetic ideas suggested by him or his life. Just as the French realized that Byron's conception of him could be filled out symbolically, the Poles and Russians saw that his historical meaning could be elaborated. Pushkin's poem essentially brings to an end the

---

[28] There was of course Bantysh-Kamensky's *Life of Mazeppa*, published in 1832, that brought together all the materials included in the *Istoria Maloi Rossii*, but it had to follow the official view of the Hetman. I have seen listed, though I have not been able to obtain, an historical romance by Piotr Ivan Golota, *Ivan Mazepa* (Moscow, 1832) that might contain some different point of view, but I doubt it. It, too, had to pass the censors. The *Ukraine: a Concise Encyclopedia* (Toronto, 1963), p. 1016, says that c. 1828 a poem, *Kochubei*, was published in Ukrainian, but I have not found a trace of it. This citation might result from confusion with Ryleev's "Kochubey," although it was written in Russian. Faddei Bulgarin wrote a novel, *Ivan Mazepa*, published in Moscow in 1833, translated into Polish in 1834, Italian in 1845, and Czech in 1854. It does not add anything new to the legend and is almost entirely unhistorical. Bulgarin was decidedly a czarist, and it was his intention to show without a doubt Mazeppa's personal and political treason. The novel was not at all successful. A good study of it appears in Gilman H. Alkire, "The Historical Novels of Faddej Bulgarin" (Ph. diss., Univ. of California, Berkeley, 1966).

legend generated by Byron's *Mazeppa* and attempts to substantiate one side of the Eastern European view of Mazeppa. Most subsequent artistic versions of the Mazeppa theme that focus on his place in history as a traitor or hero merely follow what had already been written about the theme. There is really one later treatment of Mazeppa that stands above preceding versions, and that was done by Juliusz Słowacki, the Polish émigré poet. His Mazeppa becomes a noble character in the course of the play, surpassing Byron's, Hugo's, and Pushkin's conceptions of the Hetman.

6.

JULIUSZ SŁOWACKI'S
MAZEPA

JULIUSZ SŁOWACKI'S play *Mazepa* [1] is a wholly new conception of the theme by a Romantic poet. Słowacki is not interested in the controversy over Mazeppa's heroism or treachery, or in the detailed psychology of the death-in-life experience—at least not overtly so. He conceives of Mazeppa as undergoing a metamorphosis of character from a witty, Don Juan-like courtier into a serious, angelic young man not as a result of a wild ride but of entombment alive. The focus of the play is centered on Mazeppa's moral development, so that when Mazeppa exits in Act Five he had been purified almost to sainthood.

Słowacki's works must be considered a little differently from those of Ryleev and Pushkin, because he was an *émigré* for half of his life; he lived for the most part in Western Europe from the time he was twenty-one until his death in 1849 at the age of forty. As a result, censorship was not a factor in Słowacki's work. He was also cut off from the indigenous Polish intelligentsia, and whatever he learned of current ideas in Poland and Russia came from censored newspapers, carefully worded letters from friends and family, and the incomplete and often biased information in the *émigré* circles. Among the Polish *émigré* intellectuals, he was relegated to a place beneath Adam Mickiewicz, who became the chief spokesman for many Poles in exile. Słowacki's work and personality were continually overshadowed by Mickiewicz's, and Słowacki frequently reacted bitterly and jealously to Mickiewicz's power and posi-

---

[1] To avoid confusion from the outset, I shall use this spelling of Mazeppa's name throughout this chapter only when using the title of the play. All references to the play will be from Juliusz Słowacki, *Dzieje Wszystkie*, ed. Juliusz Kleiner (Wrocław, 1958), vol. 4. I shall indicate act, scene, and lines in the text.

tion; he considered himself in competition with Mickiewicz through much of his career as a writer. To Słowacki's displeasure, he was writing for himself and a handful of exiles, though his work did on occasion reach Poland.

Although those are relevant factors to an understanding of Słowacki's work in relation to that of his contemporaries, they touch only the surface of the uniqueness of his writings. First and foremost, one must grasp some of the quality of Słowacki's imagination. He was well educated, well read, and sensitive to the point of neurosis. Słowacki's fantasies were more real to him than was the concrete world. His mind was so inhabited by visions, angels, devils, demons, and spirits that the tangible world held little truth or beauty for him. At best it was a purgatory where men suffered in order to transcend their lives and enter the world of the spirit. If Słowacki deals with the mundane—the world of facts, events, and people—he transfigures its banality.

Słowacki's imagination was fed by his reading. He knew the French and English Romantics in their original languages and studied the Bible and Homer, as well as Goethe, Schiller, Shakespeare, Racine, Calderón, Dante, and almost every other important Western writer. He assimilated all that he read to produce works that were not mere imitations but new creations that tried to surpass the originals. He sought the spirit in what he read and tried to incorporate it into what he wrote. For him literature was not merely an intellectual or aesthetic pleasure, it was an exploration of the fundamental questions of life. To read his works from the beginning—starting with the translations of Lamartine in 1825, and continuing to the great mystical works written in the late 1840s, *King Spirit* and *Genesis from the Spirit*—is to see the transformation of much of the great literature of the Western world in an evolving imagination producing works that show signs of numerous influences but that are stamped with Słowacki's unique style and ideas. Each work is a progressive step in the development of his ideas, incorporating what he had read and what he was reading at the time of its writing.

Perhaps, then, one can see how particularly difficult it is to focus upon one play by Słowacki: to look at it away from the context of his other work and to talk about it without losing some of its meaning. To reduce that difficulty to a minimum, one should consider first the pertinent works that Słowacki wrote about the same time he was working on

Mazepa, then turn to an analysis of the play, and finally to evaluate the direct major influences on it.

Before beginning, one must consider the date *Mazepa* was completed, because a problem arises from comments made by Słowacki in his correspondence. In a letter to his mother on November 7, 1834, from Geneva, he told about writing a tragedy called *Mazepa*.

Well, I danced myself out at that soiree and returned home. As luck would have it, this is the usual season [autumn] when the poetic heat falls on me—it has for the last four years without fail—for at this season I usually am creative. The next day, after the soiree, an idea came to me. The idea galloped for four hours and stopped long enough for me to consider writing five acts. Do not be surprised that it galloped, for I also thought of galloping *Mazepa*. Somehow in several days I wrote the tragedy, over which you would weep, mother; if not over Mazepa, then over me. This Mazepa will not gallop into the world this year because business is mediocre and books are not selling well. So I'll be patient. I need a year if the empty bookcases do not open. . . . Meanwhile, let *Mazepa* lie in the drawer—and if some wind should sweep me from this earth before I publish it, please inquire after this foetus (in the mother's womb) and claim it at Mrs. Pattey's. Give it to the world someday.[2]

It seems obvious from the way he writes that in some way Słowacki had been influenced by Byron's or Hugo's poems about Mazeppa, or both. Dancing reminded him of galloping which called to mind Mazeppa. No further description of this play is given anywhere. In February 1835, however, he wrote to his mother and to Eustache Januszkiewicz, an *émigré* publisher in Paris, telling them that he had just burned the manuscript of *Mazepa* in his stove: "*Mazepa* met such a sad fate." [3] The play is not mentioned in his letters until 1839, when he wrote from Paris to Antoni Woykowski, the editor of a literary weekly in Poznan, that "if it interest anyone, shortly, I shall publish a Polish tragedy entitled *Mazepa*." [4] It is difficult to say whether Słowacki really burned the manuscript in Geneva, or only pretended to and brought it out of the drawer five years later as a new work. At the time Słowacki wrote *Mazepa* he also wrote a fantasy play, *Balladyna*, on folklore motifs. He did not burn the manuscript of that play, but waited four years, until 1839, to publish it, shortly before he published *Mazepa*. If he could have saved *Balladyna* this long, could he not have done the same with *Mazepa?*

---

[2] *Korespondencja Juliusza Słowackiego*, ed., E. Sawrymowicz (Wrocław, 1962–63):267.
[3] *Ibid.*, pp. 280, 286. [4] *Ibid.*, p. 432.

The arguments of Juliusz Kleiner, the foremost Polish editor and student of Słowacki's work in this century, that Słowacki did write a tragedy *Mazepa* in Geneva but then destroyed it or burned it accidentally are convincing.[5] The Swiss *Mazepa*, as Kleiner termed it, was probably very imitative of Byron and Hugo. Słowacki would probably not have been satisfied with such a play, for he always wanted his work to transcend his sources and influences. The *Mazepa* published in 1840 is unlike any previous treatment of the theme, though it should become evident that Słowacki abstracted and transformed some basic ideas from both Byron and Hugo.[6]

Although one can find traces of techniques and ideas from Słowacki's earlier work in *Mazepa*, there is a strong resemblance to works done in 1838 and 1839, especially *Poema Piast Dantyszka* (the title means a poem about a man named Piast Dante) and *Anhelli* (this proper name is a play on the Polish word for angel).[7] In those works, Słowacki is preoccupied with the themes of pain and suffering, both on a personal and national level, and the concept of hell as he understood it from Dante. It seems significant that in his conception of hell in *Poema Piast Dantyszka*, Słowacki puts Peter I at its center.[8] Especially after the November Uprising in Poland in 1830–31, Słowacki articulated an almost violent hatred for czardom and for Nicholas I in particular. From his youth he had been a vigorous liberal, and gradually he came to see the need for political revolution for the establishment of democracy, and with the years his sense of Polish patriotism intensified. Simultaneously, his opposition grew to the monarchial system and to the aristocracy, in particular to the infighting, self-defeating Polish *szlachta* (gentry). They and the institutional

---

[5] Juliusz Kleiner, *Słowacki*, 3d ed. (Wrocław, 1958) 2:3–4.

[6] I should point out that Kazimierz J. Zimmermann, *Studium nad genezą "Mazepa"* (Lvov, 1895), p. 12, first made a case of Byron's influence, though his whole argument rests upon the letter Słowacki wrote to his mother in 1834.

[7] I disagree with Zbigniew Raszewski, one of the latest commentators on *Mazepa* in Poland, that the play is a regression from myth to history and from fantasy to the techniques of the Boulevard theaters in the development of Słowacki's ideas. See *Prace o literaturze i teatrze* (Warsaw, 1966), pp. 452–53. A great deal of criticism has been devoted to showing the possible literary influences upon *Mazepa* which I list for interest's sake. Balzac: *La Grande Bretèche*; the Dumas: *Antony, Angèle, Thérèse, Tour de Nesle*; Shakespeare: *Hamlet, Othello, Romeo and Juliet*; Hugo: *Le roi s'amuse, Lucrèce Borgia, Marion Delorme*.

[8] In a sketch of an earlier poem, *Posielenije* (*The Settlement*), from which *Poema Piast Dantyszka* developed, he also put Peter I in the center of hell.

church were the major obstacles to any successful rebellion in Poland as
Słowacki saw it; they really helped the Czar to keep the Polish nation in
chains. He came increasingly to believe that the purpose of suffering was
redemption, an obvious and old Christian concept, but one must understand that for Słowacki suffering and redemption were a part of the secular world, not the ecclesiastical one. He began to see them operating in
history, sometimes in historical characters, in mythical beings, in characters of his own creation, and in the Polish nation in general. The evil
that provoked suffering and redemption was in some cases embodied in
historical figures such as Peter I and Catherine the Great, in the institu-
tion of czardom, in Russia, in the Catholic Church, in the Polish aristocracy, and in the world in general. When Słowacki turned to history he
sometimes looked for real figures who seemed to him to be spiritually
evil people, but in most cases he looked for figures who possessed a spiritual goodness that had been obscured by their personalities or by the circumstances of history, or, as he said, he sought the "interior angel" in
men. Such a figure was a more refined version of the patriotic traitor. If
Peter I ruled the infernal regions as Słowacki conceived of them, it seems
plausible that anyone who opposed the seat of evil would not only be
heroic in a secular but also in a spiritual sense. He could be an angelic
figure through whom the forces of good would be acting. On the basis
of history, Mazeppa would be a natural figure for Słowacki to write
about because he opposed Peter I.

In the character of Mazeppa, Słowacki could bring to bear his concept
of the man whose life is a sacrificial offering for the good of the nation
and could also demonstrate his intense hatred of czardom. The battle between good and evil was the level on which he saw this historical context. The sacrificial victim is best delineated in Słowacki's odd work
Anhelli, published in 1838. It is written in a Biblical prose style and concerns the travels of an angelic character, Anhelli, through the hell of
Siberian mines where Polish exiles are dying after excruciating suffering,
to the purgatory of earth where sin and weakness reign, and finally to
the possibility of heaven where sacrifice precedes redemption. When
Anhelli falls into what is to be his final sleep, a knight appears on horseback, carrying a banner that has the word LUD (the people) written on
it. The knight announces what is to come in the future: world revolution, the falling of thrones, the triumph of the people, the resurrection of

Poland, and the new order of the "strong people." Anhelli does not know that he has been sacrificed to the great spiritual political revolution that is to come after him. As Słowacki sees it, the great revolution will not come without such preparatory sacrifices. It is not too difficult to see that Mazeppa could be considered such a victim taken from history.

Clearly, Słowacki considers Mazeppa a Pole; there is no question in his mind about Ukrainian independence; Słowacki was brought up in Krzemieniec, a town that in older times was an outpost of Polish civilization in an area populated in the main by ethnic Ukrainians. He knew Ukrainian folklore and culture and used them frequently in his works. His stepfather was a professor at the Lycée in Krzemieniec at a time when the school was a center of Ukrainian studies. Yet Słowacki did not consider the Ukraine a separate nation; to his mind, the Ukrainians were part of the Polish nation. He was not interested in finding ethnic differences between Poles and Ukrainians, for he thought in the larger terms of oppressed versus oppressor. The oppressor was Russia. The oppressed must not seek differences among themselves, but must find all means of unifying to defeat the oppressor. It is unimportant, then, to him whether or not Mazeppa was a Ukrainian; he led an attack against the Russians—that is what matters.

The goodness of Anhelli develops in the course of his wanderings; so does Mazeppa develop his in the course of the play. Mazeppa has no idea that his purification is preparation for sacrifice; the play only by implication takes up the theme of Mazeppa's future. Słowacki could, however, count on his readers to be familiar with the Mazeppa theme from history or art. When *Mazepa* ends, one knows that Peter I and Mazeppa are destined to meet at the Battle of Poltava, and that the angelic Mazeppa is not aware that he will be defeated there.

In 1834, one year before any work on the first *Mazepa*, Słowacki had already written in the Preface to his third volume of poetry:

He is mistaken who thinks that the national character of poetry consists of describing national events: events are only the cloak, the body within which the spirit of the nation or the world should be sought.[9]

The spirit could be found in Mazeppa, but probably not in 1835. In the light of *Poema Piast Dantyszka* and *Anhelli* in 1838–39, he did realize the

---

[9] Juliusz Słowacki, *Dzieła Wszystkie*, ed. Juliusz Kleiner (Wrocław, 1958) 2:12.

significance of Mazeppa's historical and spiritual opposition to Peter I and to czardom in general. For Słowacki the facts and events of history were sources of the spirit, requiring a visionary like himself to bring them to light.

Since this play is not generally known, perhaps it would be helpful to give a synopsis of the plot before proceeding with the analysis. The play is set in the castle of a Polish Palatine during the reign of Jan Kazimierz. The Palatine has been married a second time, to a young girl, Amelia. He has a son, Zbigniew, by his first marriage; he is about Amelia's age. As the play opens, the Palatine and his courtiers are awaiting the King's arrival. Lady Castellan, an older woman in the Palatine's Court, warns Amelia that Mazeppa is in company with the King and will steal her heart. Amelia is apparently a dutiful wife but is not especially happy with her old husband, while Zbigniew is very much in love with his young stepmother. Mazeppa enters the scene through a window, having become bored by the protocol of the King's arrival. When the King enters he takes more than a passing interest in Amelia. The King and Mazeppa begin to vie for Amelia's affections. The King steals under Amelia's window dressed in Mazeppa's cloak and is attacked there by Zbigniew, who slashes the King's hand, not knowing whom he has wounded. The King appeals to Mazeppa to help him out of this scandalous situation, which Mazeppa solves by slashing his own hand so that no one can tell which of the two was under Amelia's window.

In Act Two, the King tries to seduce Amelia. She openly spurns him, in no way allowing her honor to be compromised. The King becomes angry at Mazeppa for having the upper hand in this love intrigue—and, one suspects, for being generally more clever than he is—so he decides to get rid of Mazeppa by having him deliver his own death warrant to Warsaw. Mazeppa believes he is to deliver another important message for the King. Before he leaves, he meets Zbigniew, who accuses him of attempting to seduce Amelia, and they begin to fight a duel, during which the King's letter is torn open and Mazeppa learns he has been carrying his own death warrant. Mazeppa and Zbigniew end the scene as friends.

In Act Three Mazeppa enters the castle through the window of Amelia's room. He is trying to avoid being seen, so that the King will not suspect that the ruse has been discovered. Zbigniew and Amelia enter the room and Mazeppa is forced to hide in an alcove. During the scene

Zbigniew begins to declare his love for Amelia. Although she does feel for him deeply, she will not betray her duty to her husband. They are interrupted by the entrance of the Palatine, who accuses her of infidelity with Mazeppa. The rest of the act is a series of accusations and demands to know about whether or not Mazeppa is in the alcove. It is built upon multiple misunderstandings among all those present in the room but Mazeppa. Not aware that there is anyone in the alcove, Amelia swears so on a cross, but the Palatine is still dubious and orders the alcove to be bricked up, which is done immediately. Amelia subsequently realizes that someone is in the alcove and tells the Palatine, but he seals the alcove anyway and declares the room is to become the King's chapel. The Palatine does not trust Amelia at all, and her honorable intentions are now continually misunderstood.

Amelia is agonizing over her situation as Act Four opens. When Zbigniew enters her chamber and accuses her of infidelity, he believes that she was hiding Mazeppa. Zbigniew's hatred, however, is turned to a more open declaration of his love for her. She reacts by declaring she wants to die, and talks of stabbing herself. The King and the Palatine enter and the alcove is ordered torn down. The Palatine makes the King promise that he will turn the culprit inside over to him, and the King agrees. He has no idea Mazeppa is inside. Mazeppa is led out and explains what he has undergone during his entombment. The Palatine still wants revenge and Zbigniew agrees to fight Mazeppa for the family honor. They exit, a shot is heard, and Mazeppa returns. Zbigniew is dead.

Act Five is essentially a grotesque wake. The Palatine laments his son's death with increasing madness. He refuses to release Mazeppa and holds the King to his promise. Mazeppa tells Amelia that Zbigniew really committed suicide. She becomes distressed and falls on the coffin. As the Palatine's madness increases, Mazeppa comes increasingly to control the situation. The King has left and told the Palatine that he is going to lay siege to the castle. In despair, Amelia poisons herself, after realizing that Zbigniew loved her and that she really loved him. Mazeppa tells the Palatine that Zbigniew committed suicide, after which the thoroughly mad Palatine orders Mazeppa out of the castle. Mazeppa exits and the Palatine kills himself as the King's attacking army is heard approaching the death chamber.

The First Act is comical, almost farcical in places; yet it can perhaps best be described as prophetic, for the destructive machinery is set into motion in an amusingly deceptive atmosphere. Characters are casually told what will happen but they do not listen. A good case in point is Lady Castellan.

She has been criticized as a poorly conceived character because she does not seem to fit into the total pattern of the play, never reappearing after Act I, scene 10. Her role, however, is major: she is the prophetess who announces the theme of the play to Mazeppa in Act I, scene 4. "I see already, sir, that you will make this home a hell,/ That you will bring trouble through the window" (117–8). She is quite right, for Mazeppa does precipitate the tragic outcome, and he made his entrance in an earlier scene by coming through a window, the usual entrance of robbers, seducers, or spirits. Before her confrontation with Mazeppa, Lady Castellan tells Zbigniew, the Palatine's son, after meeting him for the first time, that he must be careful or he will "end up an unfaithful,/ Frivolous seducer like all army captains" (16–17). His reaction, "Heaven forbid!" is really defensive and self-incriminating. Lady Castellan has seen into his heart and found that Zbigniew loves his stepmother. In the next scene Lady Castellan meets Amelia, the Palatine's young wife, and seems to cast a spell over her, enticing her with stories of Mazeppa's fatal charms. Lady Castellan says simply that Mazeppa will fall in love with Amelia. At this point Mazeppa makes his entrance, which he describes as the moon coming through a crack in the wall and as a butterfly coming in from outside. There is something spirit-like about him, and one begins to suspect that he is some kind of Ariel, perhaps; or, keeping Lady Castellan's comments in mind, at least a man who seems to possess a demon-like quality. After confronting Zbigniew, Amelia, and Mazeppa and telling them their fate, Lady Castellan leaves the stage. She has served her purpose: that of a Cassandra who, from time to time, passes across the stage announcing doom to deaf ears. To some, perhaps, this may be giving too much significance to Lady Castellan, who might be considered no more than the informative maid or aunt in the opening scene of an Ibsen play; but Słowacki has given her too many important speeches directed at the key characters of the play to be using her in some purely mechanical way. She seems to be a charming, worldly-wise older woman who speaks in an amusing, offhand manner to everyone, but one of Słowacki's major aims in the first half of the play is to point out that the truth about people cannot be seen for the illusion that surrounds all the characters, and that the quality of that illusion is developed after Lady Castellan leaves the stage. She is the only character at the beginning of the play who sees the reality of each character's situation. She does not return to the stage because her role is taken over by Mazeppa after his conversion, and in this one way Słowacki achieves a structural balance. The interplay between truth and illusion is at the base of this tragedy.

The humor begins in the first scene, where the Palatine is waiting for King Kazimierz to arrive. He does so shortly, escorted by an entourage that is described in amusing detail by Sir Chrzastka, a courtier in the Palatine's retinue. It seems that two of the King's marshals, after a lengthy discussion about who should on protocol go through the door first, decide to enter together and get stuck in the doorway. When Chrzastka finishes his story, the Palatine orders the walls to be taken down to resolve the marshals' dispute. Lady Castellan's comment ends the scene: "Oh! What a farce!" Just so, but all the farcical elements in this scene are turned to tragic ones later, especially the symbolic walls that are erected in Act Three and torn down again in Act Four.

The second scene is entirely comic but laden with meaning. Most of the political satire is concentrated in the buffoonery here: the corrupt but amusing courtiers, the foolishness of protocol, the whimsy of the Palatine and the gentry, the total unseriousness of all these people of state and their attendants—all of which begins to form a concentrated historical fabric against which the rest of the play is enacted. Słowacki is obviously attacking the monarchy and the aristocracy. The polite language and elegant manners are frivolous and do not hide the baseness of the people using them. The decadence of the beginning turns to war in the last scene of the play. One tends to forget that as the curtain is falling King Kazimierz is about to storm the Palatine's castle, that cannonballs are flying, and that soldiers are heard shouting as they come near the death chamber where Zbigniew lies in state—another structural balance with a shift in tone.

Słowacki goes to some lengths in the first act to show that Mazeppa and King Kazimierz seem to be cut from the same cloth and that their relationship is really more that of close friends than of king and subject.

Mazeppa addresses the King very informally, often criticizing him and even belittling him. The King is also interested in winning Amelia's affections, and it is he who gets his hand slashed by Zbigniew while masquerading in Mazeppa's cloak under Amelia's window. If anything, it seems in Act One that Mazeppa is directing the King's life, that Mazeppa's is the superior mind. It need hardly be stated that the King and the court are a scandal. Kazimierz is bullied by his own page, his nobles disobey him, the court is a panorama of betrayal, vengeance, suicide, murder, foppery, and lechery in which the innocent are swept away. Mazeppa points out over and over again that the King is an ex-cardinal and woman-chaser. There is from the beginning no sense of honor among any of these people, but Słowacki does not press any of this upon the reader or viewer; it is just there in the speeches and the stage directions. Every character, except Mazeppa, is caught in the web of politics, which, it turns out, is spun by the characters' personal prejudices and flaws. Even the innocent Amelia may not be so pure. Why did she marry the old Palatine? Słowacki does not say; it is clear, however, that Amelia does not love the old man and merely fulfills her duties to him. There is no doubt that the Poland in which this play takes place is totally corrupt. The walls that are so amusingly torn down in Act One overshadow the crumbling of the Palatine's house, and once again the seemingly trivial turns to disaster, once again the illusion is pierced by a stark reality, but at this point in the play no one is aware of what awaits him. The decadent atmosphere in which these people live ultimately causes their extinction. The only one to survive is Mazeppa, but not until after he has seen through the illusions and been resurrected a new man.

As part of the spell in the castle all the male characters fall in love with Amelia. Mazeppa falls in love with her *immediately* upon seeing her but is ultimately not very affected by this love. His important scene with her in Act I, scene 9, when he tempts her to love him and she refuses, is followed by another of Lady Castellan's strange scenes. Mazeppa tells her that he has set a trap for Amelia and that the devil will take care of the rest. He speaks here, too, as though he were in league with some demonic power of which Lady Castellan is aware. He remains in the power of this seemingly evil spirit until after his entombment in Act Three. Amelia's description of his stealing a kiss in the garden reminds one of a typical country girl's encounter with someone she thinks is the devil—

the kind of devil one finds in folk legends. She tells the King about the
kiss and he tries to seduce her in the course of the scene. Mazeppa's
demonic quality is further explored in his scene with Zbigniew in Act
Two, which one expects to end in *Brüderschaft* but turns out quite differently. Mazeppa says:

> Finally—and I confess this
> Humbly—I am moved to contrition;
> I'm ashamed of the role I've played in this castle:
> So if you permit, dear Zbigniew,
> Let us part in peace and embrace like brothers.
> There was some kind of spell in this castle, in the
>   moon, in the garden
> That confused me, made my love turn passionate;
> The spell continues and humbles me before you
> And makes me feel sincere affection for you.
>
> (II, ix, 224–32)

To be sure, there is a spell and it has not been broken yet. In his soliloquy in the next scene, Mazeppa seems unable to understand his broth-
erly affection for Zbigniew. Why did he have a change of heart?

> Mazeppa! Now your colors are different—
> What happened to your gilded mask?
> You spoke like a priest—the devil called in vain:
>   *Haro!*
> You wallowed in virtue as though it were mud, you
>   didn't care about yourself. . . .
> Two days of this kind of humor and I'll die. I'll be
> Sitting in heaven up to my ears. Ha! The devil will
>   return.
>
> (II, ix, 325–30)

In this speech one senses that Mazeppa is possessed by some dark power,
but Słowacki does not seem to want to suggest anything like the overt li-
aison between Faust and the devil; he prefers Mazeppa's connection with
evil to be more like Macbeth's, though even less explicit. Mazeppa's different colors and "gilded mask" suggest also that he has been playing a
role. He has for the first time in the play allowed his genuine feelings to
come through, and he has for a few minutes stopped playing the game of
illusions being acted out by everyone in the Palatine's castle. Słowacki

endows Mazeppa with some degree of demonic power to suggest the evil in every man, but more important, perhaps, to imply that Mazeppa's life is guided by some power outside of himself, a power that Lady Castellan sees and that Mazeppa merely feels from time to time.

Act Three, that mysterious act in which everyone misunderstands everyone else and the wrong man is entombed, is the center and main symbol of the play. Very significant is the conversion of the alcove in Amelia's room into a tomb that functions as an altar where Mass is said. The Palatine walls in Mazeppa in an attempt to isolate the trouble in his house. He is mistaken, however, in believing that Mazeppa loves Amelia at this point; his son Zbigniew has been in love with her. When Mazeppa is entombed he knows the truth about everyone there: Amelia and Zbigniew are in love, the Palatine suspects Mazeppa, and the King, to cover his own feelings for Amelia, passes his guilt onto Mazeppa. The one man who could right all the wrongs is the one who is not able to tell his story. The complexity of meaning of the entombment is astounding. At the crucial point in the play Słowacki removes the main character from the stage, though his presence is felt and all action revolves about him.

When the tomb-altar is torn down in Act Four, Mazeppa emerges saying, "My King, I come out from the altar/ Like Lazarus—I shall expose all as it was." As Lady Castellan had in the First Act, Mazeppa now assumes the role of prophet. What happened inside the tomb-altar is Mazeppa's transfiguration. Whatever demons possessed him before are gone; his evil nature has been shed; he now sees the illusions and the reality. The tomb was first a prison where he almost died, suggesting first the archetypal experience of Byron's Mazeppa and second, perhaps, the inner freedom that a prisoner comes to understand as Byron's Bonnivard did in "The Prisoner of Chillon." But then the tomb is an altar, a sanctified place. Mazeppa tells the story of Amelia's pet canary, which was trapped with him. When the canary died of lack of air, Mazeppa fainted. First of all, that bird, like the raven in Byron's *Mazeppa* and the songbird in "Chillon," symbolizes the return to life, but since the bird is associated with Amelia, it may also signify the death of her in Mazeppa's heart, and ultimately her own death; and on a yet higher level, the bird must be associated with the Mass and the Holy Spirit. The large symbolism of the Mass—the death followed by resurrection—is the analogue for Mazeppa's great transfiguration. Słowacki is not suggesting that Mazeppa is Christ, a hasty conclusion that some critics might come to; instead, he probably has in mind the more general Pauline doctrine of the "new man" transformed on the road to Damascus.

The analogue for that experience becomes in a broad Christian sense a deep personal experience that turns a man toward the path of good somewhat akin to the "necessary death" of Orestes in Goethe's *Iphegenia in Tauris*—where the hero is also "born again" to begin a new life—or the new life of Orestes in the *Eumenides*. The Mazeppa who emerges from the tomb in Act Four is such a "new man," and whatever was diabolic in him has been transformed into the angelic.

What is disconcerting about the new Mazeppa is that he seems to have little effect upon the lives of the people around him. He is almost a bystander to the tragic events that envelop Amelia, Zbigniew, and the Palatine in the rest of the play. The point is that the darker side of these peoples' lives has now been unleashed and they have not undergone the experience, any experience, to make them new people. Mazeppa, like St. Michael, watches over the apocalypse of their lives as it unfolds around him. If he is anything like Słowacki's Anhelli, Mazeppa is not necessarily aware of the effect he may have upon others.

Mazeppa's inability to help them is perhaps best illustrated in the theme of honor that runs through the whole play and converges in these crucial scenes. It was, after all, for Amelia's honor that Mazeppa was entombed and to save her honor that he was freed. The Palatine, however, is driven by some wild instinct to make Mazeppa pay for *thinking* of dishonoring his wife; the Palatine, like everyone but Amelia, seems to be unaware that Mazeppa has changed. The Palatine's irrationality about Mazeppa may be partially explained by a remark by Zbigniew that is never commented upon in the play, but that like so many other remarks has portentous implications. When Zbigniew is pleading with his father to spare Amelia in Act Three, he says among more topical things,

> Father, your son swears on his immortal soul
> That there is no one there—is that not enough for you?
> Father! It will be with me as it was with my brother
> Whom you killed unintentionally years ago. . . .

> (158–62)

Is the house of the Palatine cursed with this crime that must be expiated? Does a Fury lurk on the housetop? Is the Palatine a barbarian who has just learned the manners of the court? His blindly seeking revenge against Mazeppa, who has not dishonored Amelia, has no motivation unless it is linked in some way with primal revenge that lurks behind the play. Honor becomes, in the light of all the misunderstandings about it in the play, a dangerous *courtoisie;* it is a matter of etiquette rather than morality. This seems to be Słowacki's point about the historical context of the play. Mazeppa is the only character who understands the morality of honor after his ordeal; the others, the King included, are adhering to a more primitive code based on blind revenge and deception. Mazeppa is the new man who realizes that he cannot affect the old code, which must destroy itself. Such is the Poland of the mid-seventeenth century as Słowacki sees it. Mazeppa must leave it behind.

The fifth act, sometimes considered the most French because it is filled with the *grotesquerie* Hugo believed was essential to Romantic drama, brings to an end the house of the Palatine and the extinction of the curse or spell. The Palatine openly defies the King by insisting on holding Mazeppa hostage. The Palatine's vengeance congeals into madness. His speech in Act Five, scene 8, fuses the important imagery associated with him: the Furies, Orestes-like, have invaded his mind; the demons that plagued Mazeppa earlier appear to have possessed the Palatine, but much more intensely.

> They take him—they tie him—it is I. It is vengeance!
> The ropes cut deep into the meat . . . the horse rends
>   the flesh.—
> I'm cold.—Son! Your father drags himself in blood,
>   but
> Do not be afraid of the bloody ghost. . . .
> What is that?—How dark it is. . . . What kinds of
>   monsters
> Are kissing loudly in the dark corridor?—
> Come out of the casket—come out hideous wretch.
> Say it is not true. . . . Tell the boards to warp!
> Stand! Open coffin! I am ready to forgive
> If you beg on your knees. My tears are ready to
>   flow. . . .
> Oh coffin, I am ready to forgive you—I, your father,
> If you weep for my wretchedness.—

Away corpses! Let the devils drive you through the
                                   fire!
Enough betrayals! Enough life!

                                    (200–13)

    The Palatine's opening words sound like a prophecy of what is in store for Mazeppa, recalling Pasek's *Memoirs* and Byron's *Mazeppa*. These lines, of course, apply to the Palatine himself. He has been lashed to his own vengeance, unable to get free until he is ridden to death. He has no absolution like Mazeppa, no death-in-life experience. The energy and speed of the fantastic ride described by Byron and then by Hugo, a ride that Mazeppa has not yet experienced in Słowacki's play, is transformed in *Mazepa* in two ways: up to his entombment Mazeppa is under a spell that drives his passions wild, that distorts his sense of reality, but after his experience in the tomb-altar the fury comes to reside in the Palatine's vengeance. It wears itself out as the horse wore itself out, exhausted by the excess of its force.

    The radically new direction the play takes after Mazeppa's entombment is best explained in terms of Mazeppa's character. Słowacki made the center of his play as disruptive and unusual as he could in the visual, dramatic, and symbolic senses to indicate the fantastic transformation of his central character. In order for the change to seem plausible its cause had to be almost a miracle. But Słowacki would not tolerate a *deus ex machina*, so he relies upon symbolism and religion to make his point. Mazeppa's new role in the play is stated by him when he addresses the mad Palatine:

Your son's body is suffering,
He does not want to feel you under him—he moans in
                              the coffin.
Stand up from the coffin, insulter of the dead, and
                        fall on your face,
For I am their avenging angel . . .
Because I have lightning on my lips. It is only
                    because of my mercy that
I do not hurl it at your poor, grey head,
Your wretched head. . . .

                                (V, vii, 189–94)

    The charming courtier had turned into the avenging angel, the moral avenger, an apocalyptic figure. The course of the play has been his education and purgation, almost as though he were being prepared for the role he is going to play in the history of Eastern Europe. When Mazeppa leaves the stage at the end of the play, he says that he will meet whatever lies beyond the threshold, and one knows that it is a great deal more than has transpired in this play. Suffering brings strength that will allow him to endure greater suffering. His newly realized morality establishes him as a worthy leader. Słowacki gives the very strong impression that though Mazeppa may have once, in his youth, been a licentious courtier, after he underwent the ordeal of almost dying he emerged a strong, honorable figure.

As pointed out earlier, many sources and analogues have been proposed for *Mazepa*, but there seem to be really only three central sources of inspiration: Jan Pasek's *Memoirs*, published in 1836, and Byron's and Hugo's poems about Mazeppa. The *Memoirs* are a mixture of anecdote and fact that describe, among many aspects of Polish life in the seventeenth century, the decadence of the Court of Jan Kazimierz. The story of Mazeppa's supposed affair with Countess Falbowska and his subsequent dramatic banishment from Poland became public knowledge in Eastern Europe with the publication of the *Memoirs*. In many of the previous artistic treatments of Mazeppa, emphasis was placed upon his love intrigues, which were generally negative and related in various ways to his seemingly equivocal political action. Pasek includes in the *Memoirs* a short poem that sums up such a view of Mazeppa.

> *Adulterium* and fraudulent talents
> You see, Mazeppa, as the commerce of fickleness:
> To lie foully and to steal what the nobleman left behind!
> How unpleasant it is to turn the other cheek.
> The King trained you for honor.
> Falbowski was grooming you for knighthood
>
> Honored sir, you know how pleasant
> It is to have an understanding husband!
> You were sick with the itch of flesh,
> But an effective prescription was prepared for you:
> The paradise of another home is very dear,
> For such a defect there are paradisal spurs.[10]

---

[10] I have not done justice to this little poem in my translation, which has many plays on words in Polish. *Pamietniki Jana Chryzostoma Paska*, ed. Bronisław Gubrynowicz (Lvov, 1898), p. 226.

If it is part of Słowacki's intention to show the metamorphosis of Mazeppa's character into an angelic figure, then it is not surprising that he
would write about a love situation in young Mazeppa's life, for it was in
precisely such a situation that Mazeppa was accused of impropriety and
treachery, an accusation that Słowacki might wish to show to be false.
Pushkin, for instance, made much of Mazeppa's deception of Maria. It
seems obvious, as the Polish critic Zbigniew Raszewski has pointed out,
that Słowacki was trying to whitewash Mazeppa's character.[11]

Słowacki chooses to write about a time in Mazeppa's life that antedates
any previous artistic treatment of him. Clearly, Mazeppa is a fickle lover
at the opening of the play, but when he exits in Act Five he is a su-
premely good person. The implication is that the "avenging angel" could
and would not act improperly during the rest of his life. Historically
considered, Mazeppa has fifty years to live after he exits in Act Five,
fifty years of complicated personal and political involvement. If Mazeppa
were really, i.e. historically, the angelic character Słowacki conceived,
then there is no question of his becoming a traitor. He would have to
have been motivated by good rather than evil after his metamorphosis.
By establishing Mazeppa's profound virtue in the Hetman's youth, Słowacki probably thought that he could vindicate the rest of Mazeppa's
life: once converted to the forces of good, Mazeppa could not join the
forces of evil.

Słowacki doubtless had Pasek's *Memoirs* in mind in *Mazepa* because he
makes the nobleman a minor character. For some reason, not stated in
the play, Mazeppa dislikes and avoids him. Mazeppa, explaining to Lady
Castellan in the first act why he chose not to make his entrance with the
King's entourage, says:

> In the doorway is Sir Pasek,
> Like a three-headed Cerebus—my blood stops in my
>   veins. . . .[12]

Throughout the play Mazeppa avoids Pasek whenever he can. It was
known from the *Memoirs* that Pasek and Mazeppa had a misunder-
standing, and Słowacki gives the impression in the play that these two

---

[11] Zbigniew Raszewski, "Słowacki i Mickiewicz wobec teatru romantycznego," *Pamiętnik
Teatralny* (1959, I–III, 12), p. 431.
[12] *Dziela*, 4:202. Act I, iv, 113–16.

are at odds from the beginning. Pasek is a lackey and hanger-on in the play, always waiting on the King. It is apparent from Pasek's character in the play that Słowacki did not believe his account.

Mazepa has an unusual structure and tone, moving from farce to tragedy, which parallels Mazeppa's change of character from rakish courtier to honorable man. Lines and characters may at first seem ridiculous but become profound, and the play continually shifts between the serious and the melodramatic. *Mazepa* sometimes seems to hang at an uncomfortable angle between melodrama and tragedy, a dilemma for so many critics who find themselves apologizing for it.[13] The play, however, is not so strange in the light of the work of Kleist, Pirandello, Ionesco, Brecht, or Pinter. Słowacki had a sense of the absurd that manifests itself best in comic scenes, but that also surfaces in the tragic scenes in either grotesque or serious comedy-of-errors situations. *Mazepa* is highly structured and the shift in tone is necessary to the development of the meaning of the play.

That development is understood better by seeing how the play relates to Hugo's and Byron's versions of the Hetman. Byron's poem centers about Mazeppa's almost dying on the back of a horse, while Hugo's focuses on the ride as ultimately the rising of the imagination of the poet-king. Hugo's Mazeppa undergoes a poetic "resurrection" while Byron's is vengeful and amoral. Słowacki places the experience of almost dying at the center of his play, too, not on a horse's back but in the tomb that is built and destroyed on the stage. Słowacki transfers the same ordeal into a new set of images, extracting what seemed to him to be crucial action in the previous two works and putting it into a new context. The situation is archetypally the same, but Mazeppa is resurrected in a religious sense in Słowacki's play.

Because Słowacki is writing for the theater he can use symbols that are concrete, that are before the spectators' eyes, and that do not have to be imagined. Słowacki seemed very impressed with Hugo's symbolic metamorphosis of Mazeppa and wanted to achieve the same thing, but using, of course, a different set of symbols and situations. Słowacki is not interested in Mazeppa as an artist or genius; he wants his Mazeppa to un-

---

[13] See Edward Csato, *Szkice o dramatach Słowackiego* (Warsaw, 1960), pp. 281–84; Jan Kott, *Miarka za miarkę* (Warsaw, 1962), pp. 164–70.

dergo a conversion, a conversion in the broad Christian sense. Whereas Hugo wanted his Mazeppa to soar beyond the mundane on the back of Genius, Słowacki wants his hero to become an avenging angel. Słowacki likes the supranatural quality with which Hugo has endowed his Mazeppa, but he turns that quality to the supernatural. For the first time since the Baroque apotheosis of Mazeppa in art in the late seventeenth and early eighteenth centuries, a moral-religious quality is given the Hetman. The tomb and his conversion are what the whole play is about: all early action points to it; all subsequent action leads from it. The tone and structure are built around the significance of the central symbol and experience, which are so affecting, so cataclysmic that what follows them must be drastically altered.

No treatment of Mazeppa before of after Słowacki's raised him to such heroic stature. Byron, Ryleev, and Pushkin tried in their works to resolve the Hetman's character in terms of the historical data they had at hand. Byron, fascinated and disgusted by man's refusal to learn from history, used the Hetman as an example of passion and selfishness that was doomed to fail. Ryleev and Pushkin used Mazeppa to try to resolve problems of nationality anf revolutionary independence. Even Zaleski, though tossing aside Pasek's estimate of the Hetman and creating a totally fictional set of circumstances to explain Mazeppa's motivation, wanted to create a character to vindicate Polish history. Of Słowacki's predecessors only Hugo saw Mazeppa out of the context of history and interpreted his experience in purely subjective but artistic terms. History matters to Słowacki but in a larger sense. He does not care about borders, treaties, battles, and strategies; it is the soul of a nation, the soul of its people and leaders that he is trying to expose. The world of the senses is only a cloak for the all-important spirit. So Słowacki sees Mazeppa as virtuous, but as a human being he has to be purified of the evil in his environment and himself in order to become a great leader. His Mazeppa is not ultimately Byronic, though up to his entombment he seems to be; he is a visionary at the end of the play. He will not be deluded by the false again.

Słowacki, however, is most interested in raising Mazeppa above the plane of political history into the supernatural. When Mazeppa exits at the end of the play, he had the makings of the proper sacrificial victim as Słowacki conceived him in *Anhelli*. Mazeppa, the avenging angel, can move through history toward his grand confrontation with the evil Czar Peter I that will spell his physical doom. However, Mazeppa's spirit will transcend death: his life will not have been in vain, for it will become part of the necessary suffering preceding the ultimate resurrection of a liberated Poland. History has been transformed into hagiography by Słowacki; a historical figure had been raised to secular sainthood. Only Słowacki conceived of Mazeppa in this messianic-mystical way, and no other treatment of the Hetman in the West or the East made him any greater than Słowacki did.

CONCLUSION

MAZEPPA did not disappear from art after Słowacki's play. The theme passed into music in the form of a piano étude and a tone poem by Liszt, inspired primarily by Hugo's and Byron's poems but not by Vernet's painting; and, of course, Tchaikovsky turned *Poltava* into an opera, *Mazeppa*, which is rarely done outside of Russia. In the 1850s and 1860s, the Mazeppa theme was a favorite in equestrian theaters and circuses, especially in the United States, and in puppet shows across Europe. All of these later versions of the theme, including such twentieth-century works as Bertolt Brecht's ballad "Mazeppa" and Roy Campbell's poem on the theme, are inspired by or imitative of their Romantic antecedents.

The Mazeppa theme reached a richness and complexity in the Romantic period in Europe because it embodied meanings that were significant to Romantic artists. The Western legend, first sketched in Voltaire's *Histoire de Charles XII*, was developed and enlarged in the works of Dorville, Byron, Géricault, Delacroix, Vernet, Rességuier, Boulanger, and finally Hugo into an increasingly symbolic figure. For the Romantics in Western Europe, Mazeppa's life and experiences suggested a heroic struggle for political freedom and by extension for artistic freedom in the face of oppression, and threw into relief the often frustrating or adverse results of the struggle that seemed so evident to the idealists who lived during or just after the French Revolution, the rise and fall of Napoleon, and the aftermath of the Congress of Vienna. At a time when politics and art were close, if only in the minds of so many artists who were caught up in the dramatic events of the early nineteenth century, Mazeppa could conveniently embody their artistic anguish and aspirations in a quasi-political context. For them fact moved toward legend, history toward art, and both became transformed into myths or symbols. In so many ways Mazeppa seems like Prometheus, one of the Romantics' favorite mythological sufferers. They, however, sought the Promethean in a human being, like Mazeppa, and tried to raise him to titanic heights. Their concern was no longer to bring the gods to Earth, but rather to elevate man to the heavens.

In Poland and Russia one sees similar processes at work on the theme, but in the cases of Ryleev and Pushkin the emphasis was heavily on fact and history, which nonetheless became legendary in their poems, though not symbolic. Słowacki, seeing history as a paradigm for cosmology, placed Mazeppa in his grand design of the evolution of the messianic heroes who, he firmly believed, would eventually triumph over evil.

Mazeppa's use in European Romanticism is at once the story of a minor figure who captured the imagination of many important artists and of an unbroken chain of artistic influence and inspiration. As a result, one can see the Romantics' minds at play with a subject that had wide and deep cultural appeal throughout Europe in the Romantic period.

AFTERTHOUGHTS

I SHOULD LIKE to close this study of Ivan Mazeppa in European Romanticism by making a few comments about what some critics call the Romantic imagination. By understanding how one figure was utilized by Romantic artists in different ways, one can, perhaps, see a little more clearly some of the qualities considered characteristic of the Romantic mind: gothicism, new uses and meanings of history, the transformation of subject from one art form to another, the preoccupation with the artist in society and with the creative process, the emphasis on individual suffering (which moves from *Ichschmerz* toward the spiritual or mystical), and the relation of politics to art. Although these characteristics existed to varying degrees in artists of different countries at slightly different times, there is a general sense that Romanticism as a movement underwent an evolution in Europe between 1789, to use a convenient though imprecise date, and 1840. It seems to me that, for better or worse, the end point of that evolution, reflected in the matured Romantic imagination, is messianic mysticism.

The Romantics were extremely interested in liberators who could deliver nations from political oppression, an interest prompted no doubt by their contemporary history and political idealism. Such liberators, the Romantics felt, had to be tried and refined by suffering in order to be purified for their messianic task. Often the Romantics looked to myth and history for their examples, or, like Blake, they created new myths. The suffering of the liberators, or heroes, was usually beyond the range of human experience; or, perhaps more aptly, what the Romantics thought and felt was usually beyond the range of human experience. Such suffering gave these heroes a special spiritual character in the minds of the Romantics, and often, as a result, they so appeared in Romantic art. That special quality can be called, in a broad sense, mystical. Since many Romantics shied away from institutional religions, the quality of the mysticism in their works often seems areligious. It is a mysticism that acknowledged a spiritual dimension in man that can work either good or evil, though the Romantics generally tended to avoid such orthodox classifications of the spirit. Very few were able to accept the total goodness of the human spirit, though such total acceptance seemed to be the point of a good deal of Romantic art and philosophy. Notable exceptions are Blake, the late Słowacki, and Krasiński. The mysticism that most often appears in Romantic art, then, resembles the implicit Christianity of Job, Eccelesiastes, and the Sermon on the Mount with variations of gnosticism. The work of Blake, the late Wordsworth, and the late Shelley was mystical in this way. Słowacki and Mickiewicz carried the mystical in their work to a maturity equalling if not surpassing Blake's.

Mazepa is an example of the mystical-messianic in Słowacki's work, though it is not so evident as in his later works. The only earlier instance of a similar view of Mazeppa is in Dorville's *Memoires d'Azéma*, where Mazeppa's arrival in the Ukraine is considered a sign of salvation by the peasants. But in that novel one senses that it is the superstitious belief of the peasants that matters and not what the rationalists, such as the generals, make of it. In the novel Mazeppa appears as a sensitive man who develops into a strong political leader; he does not consider himself a salvific figure in the novel as he does in Słowacki's play. The novel keeps the historical figure on the political plane whereas the play moves him up to the mystical-messianic.

So many of the Romantics who turned to history and historical figures as a kind of secular substitute for religion and faith in Providence ended up turning history and its great men into new gods, saints, and angels. This is, of course, not a clear line of development, but there is a sense that as Romanticism matured (and its maturity includes its progress across Europe from England to Russia) its chief characteristics (like the interest in history, landscapes, heroes, and art) took on increasingly more mystical qualities. The treatment of Mazeppa by Słowacki is along the road to this kind of development.

APPENDIX

Ivan Mazeppa In Works of Art and Literature (1688—1840)

1688   "Muza Roxolanska, o triumfalnej slawie i fortunie hetmana Mazepy," by Ivan Ornovsky; a panegyric published in Polish in Chernihiv. Included is an engraving and coat of arms of Mazeppa by Ivan Shchersky.

1689   *Echo głosu wolającego na puszczy*, by Stefan Yavorsky; a book of panegyrics published in Latin and Polish in Chernihiv. Included is an engraving and coat of arms of Mazeppa by Ivan Shchersky.

1690   "Illustrissima ac Magnificentissima Domino D. Johanni Mazeppa, Duci Exercitum" by Stefan Yavorsky; a panegyric in Latin.

1695   *Alcides Rossyski, triumfalnym laurem ukoronowany* by Filip Orlik; panegyrics published in Polish and Latin in Vilna. Included is an engraving and coat of arms of Mazeppa by Ivan Shchersky.

       An allegorical portrait of Mazeppa by Leontii Tarasevich.

1698   "Hippomenes Sarmacki," by Filip Orlik; a panegyric published in Polish in Kiev. The poem is part of a collection of panegyrics in Latin and Polish, *Slava Shermety*. Included in the volume is an engraving and coat of arms of Mazeppa by Leontii Tarasevich.

1699   *Theatrum perennis gloriae*, by Ivan Ornovsky; panegyrics in Latin published in Chernihiv.

c. 1700   A portrait by Zakhary Samoilovich (?).

c. 1703   A portrait by Zakhary Samoilovich (?).

1704   First anti-Mazeppa Ukrainian folk songs and poems begin to appear. They concern Mazeppa's strange dealings with Semen Palia.

1705   *Vladimir*, by Feofan Prokopovich; a play written in a combination of Church Slavonic and vernacular Russian languages. After 1709, Prokopovich eliminated references to Mazeppa in the prologue and epilogue.

1706   An allegorical painting by Ivan Migur.

1708   A translation of the New Testament into Arabic with an elaborate coat of arms of Mazeppa.

       A large allegorical portrait by Daniel Goliahovsky.

Three poems allegedly written by Mazeppa:
"Vsi pokoiu shchyre proknut"
"Oj, bida, bida"
"Bidna moja golovonka"
A doctoral thesis in philosophy dedicated to Mazeppa by Ivan Novytsky.

1709   The last of sixteen anti-Mazeppa, pro-Palia folk songs and poems appear.

c. 1710   *In vit aperium Mazepae*, by Ivan Ornovsky; anti-Mazeppa poems in Latin.

1764   André Constant Dorville's novel, *Memoires d'Azéma, contenant diverses anecdotes des règnes de Pierre le Grand, Empéreur de Russie et de l'Impératrice Catherine son Épouse* (Amsterdam). A second French edition appeared in 1766. Translated into Danish: *Azemas et Russik Fruentemmeis forunderlige Tildragelser* (1769); into German: *Die schone Russinn oder wunderbare Geschichte der Azema* (Braunschwig, 1766 and 1773); and translated from German into Russian: *Prekrasnaja Rosianka* (Moscow, three editions between 1784 and 1796).

1775   A portrait, *Mazepae aetatis 70*, by Jean Pierre Norblin.

1796   A portrait of Mazeppa by Daniel Beye from an earlier engraving by Samuel Falk.

1803   *Pułtawa; poemat epiczny*, by Nicodemus Muśnicki, S.J.; an epic poem published in Polish in Warsaw.

1811   A play about Mazeppa supposed to have been performed in America and written by Aleksei Griogorovich Evstafiev. The play has not been found.

1812   *Alexis Petrovich: ein romantisch-historische Trauerspiel in fünf Akten*, by Heinrich Bertuch; a play published in Gotha.

1815   *The Cossack: a Poem, in Three Cantos*, by Robert Etty; published in London.

1819   *Mazeppa*, by Lord Byron; published in London, Paris, and Boston.

1820   *Mazeppa Travestied: a Poem*, with an introductory address to the goddess of "Milling," and her worshipper, "The Fancy"; published in London.

1822   An engraving of Mazeppa by A. Osipov in Bantysh-Kamensky's *Istoria Maloi Rossii . . .* published in Moscow.
A sketch for a play about Mazeppa by Kondraty Ryleev.

1823   A lithograph of Mazeppa by Theodore Géricault. A drawing of Mazeppa (1820–24), perhaps a study for the published lithograph.
Two *dumas*, "Peter the Great in Ostrogiska" and "Kochubey," by Kondraty Ryleev.
An anonymous play, *Mazeppa; or the Wild Horse of the Ukraine*, was performed in London at the Royal Cobourg Theater. No text preserved.

1824   An imitation of Géricault's *Mazeppa* by Eugene Delacroix. Two original sketches on the theme. A painting, *Les imprécations de Mazeppa*, sometimes called *Mazeppa attaché au cheval sauvage*. There are eight sketches for this painting.
A *duma* about Mazeppa written in Polish by Bohdan Zaleski.

1825   Fragments of a long poem, *Mazeppa*, and a published one, *Voynarovsky*, by Kondraty Ryleev; published in St. Petersburg.
An equestrian drama, *Mazeppa ou le cheval Tartare, mimodrame en trois actes*, by Jean Cuvelier de Trie and Leopold A. Chandenson, at the Cirque Olympique in Paris.
John Howard Payne adapted the Cuvelier-Chandenson drama as *Mazeppa, or the Wild Horse of Tartary, an equestrian melodrama in three acts for American audiences*. This is the date found on the ms., but it probably was not produced in America until 1831.

1826   A painting, *Mazeppa aux loups*, and a second version, *Mazeppa enchaîné*, by Horace Vernet.

1827   A painting, *Le Supplice de Mazeppa*, by Louis Boulanger. A second painting (date uncertain), *Le Mort du Cheval de Mazeppa*. A lithograph of the first was made by Bès and Dubreuil and reprinted in 1855.

"Kochubey," a short story (?), by E. Aladin, published in Russia.

1828   A Ukrainian poem, "Kochubei." (?)

1829   "Mazeppa," a lyric poem in *Tableaux poétiques* by Jules de Rességuier; published in Paris.

"Mazeppa," a lyric poem in *Les Orientales*, by Victor Hugo; published in Paris.

1830   An anonymous novel, *Mazeppa, chef des Cosaques de l'Ukraine. Roman historique sous le règne de Pierre le Grand, impér. De Russie at Jean Casimir, roi de Pologne;* published in Paris.

1831   A lithograph by Leroy, published in Paris. Ths is probably the work of Louis Joseph Leroy (1812–85), the French engraver and landscape painter, or Joseph Anne Jules Leroy (1812–60) the Belgian painter, or Pierre François Charles Leroy (1803–33), the French painter.

Mazeppa; or, the Wild Horse of Tartary, A Romantic drama, in 3 acts dramatized from Lord Byron's poem, by H. M. Milner, first performed at the Royal Amphitheatre, Westminister Bridge, on Easter Monday of that year.

1832   A historical romance, *Ivan Mazepa*, by Piotr Ivan Golota; published in Moscow.

1833   A novel, *Mazeppa*, by Faddei Venediktovich Bulgarin; published in Moscow. Translated into Polish (1834), Italian (1845), and Czech (1854).

A lithograph of Mazeppa by Alexander Ludwig Molinari after Vernet's painting.

Performances of the *Mazeppa*'s Milner and Payne at the Bowery and Amphitheater in Richmond Hill, New York.

An etching by Reveil of an original painting by A. Colin illustrating lines from section IX of Byron's *Mazeppa*.

1838   A ballet *Mazeppa ossia il cavallo sevaggio* done in Venice.

1839   Juliusz Słowacki's play, *Mazepa;* published (in Polish) in Paris.

A SELECTED BIBLIOGRAPHY

Aimé-Azam, Dénise. *Mazeppa, Géricault et son temps.* Paris, 1954.

Allen, W. E. D. *The Ukraine; a History.* Cambridge, England: The University Press, 1941.

Aristide, Marie. *Le Peintre Poète Louis Boulanger.* Paris, 1925.

Aronson, M. " 'Konrad Vallenrod' i 'Poltava,' " *Vremennik Pushkinskoe Komissii* 2 (1936): 43–56.

Bantysh-Kemensky, Dmitrii Nikolaevich. *Istoriia Maloi Rossii ot vodvoreniia slavian v sei stran do prisoedineniia onoi, v 1654 godi, k rossiiskomu gosudarstvi tsarem Aleksem Mikhailovichem.* Moscow, 1822.

——. *Zhizn Mazepy.* Moscow, 1832.

Baudelaire, Charles. *Oeuvres complètes.* Paris, 1961.

Beauplan, Guillaume le Vasseur. *Déscription de l'Ukraine depuis les confines de la Moscovie jusqu'aux limites de la Transylvanie.* Paris, 1861.

Bengesco, Georges. *Voltaire: Bibliographie de ses oeuvres.* Paris, 1882.

Bertuch, Heinrich Friedrich Christian. *Alexis Petrowitch: ein romantische-historische Trauerspiel in fünf Akten.* Gotha, 1812.

Borschak, Elie. "Early Relations Between England and Ukraine." *The Slavonic and East European Review* 10 (June 1931): 138–60.

——. "Histoire de L'Ukraine: publications en langue ukrainienne parues en dehors de l'U.S.S.R." *Revue Historique* 187 (1939): 1–30.

——. *La Légende historique de l'Ukraine 'Istorija Rusov.'* Paris, 1949.

——. "L'Ukraine dans la littérature de l'Europe occidentale." *Le Monde Slave* 3 (Paris, 1933): 120–41, 300–15; 4: 141–59, 421–43; 1 (1934): 467–78; 2: 136–47; 4: 126–51, 305–20; 1 (1935): 294–313, 449–74.

——. "Mazepa liudina istorichnij diiach." *ZNTS* (Lvov), 152.

——. "Nevidomij francuz'kij roman XVIII stolitta pro Mazepa." *Nova Hromada* (Vienna) 1:55–61.

——. "Voltaire et L'Ukraine." *Ukrajna* (Kiev), 1.

—— et René Martel. *Vie de Mazeppa.* Paris, 1931.

Bray, René. *Chronologie du romantisme (1804–1830).* Paris, 1963.

Brewster, Dorothy. *East-West Passage: A Study in Literary Relationships.* London: Allen & Unwin, 1954.

Brion, Marcel. *Romantic Art.* New York: McGraw-Hill, 1960.

Brumfitt, J. H. *Voltaire: Historian.* London: Oxford University Press, 1958.

Byron and Byroniana: A Catalogue of Books. London: Mathews, 1930.

Byron, George Gordon, Lord. *The Works of Lord Byron. Poetry.* Ed. by Ernest Hartley Coleridge. London: Heinemann, 1899.

Byron, George Gordon, Lord. *The Works of Lord Byron: with his Letters and Journals and his Life,* by Thomas Moore, Esq. London, 1832.

——. *The Complete Poetical Works of Byron.* Ed. by Paul E. More. Boston: Houghton Mifflin, 1935.

——. *The Works of Lord Byron: Letters and Journals.* Ed. by Rowland E. Prothero. London: John Murray, 1898–1901.

Calvert, William J. *Byron: Romantic Paradox.* New York: Russell & Russell, 1962.

Carpenter, Frederic Ives. *Selections from the Poetry of Lord Byron.* New York: H. Holt & Co., 1900.

Churchill, John and Awnsham. *Collection of Voyages and Travels.* London, 1704.

Clément, Charles. *Géricault: étude biographique et critique avec le catalogue raisonée de l'oeuvres du maître.* Paris, 1868.

Clinton, George. *Memoire of the Life and Writings of Lord Byron.* London, 1831.

Coleman, Marian Moore. *Mazeppa: Polish and American: A Translation of Słowacki's 'Mazepa', together with a brief survey of Mazeppa in the U.S.* Cheshire, Conn.: Cherry Hill Books, 1966.

——. "Mazeppa, Traitor or 'Splendid Rebel.' " *Alliance Journal* 9 (1959): 18–27.

Conservateur Littéraire 3 (Dec. 1820): 212–16.

Cross, Samuel H. and Ernest J. Simmons. *Alexander Pushkin: His Life and Literary Heritage.* New York: The American Russian Institute for Cultural Relations with the Soviet Union, 1937.

Csato, Edward. *Szkice o dramatach Słowackiego.* Warsaw, 1960.

Dédieu, Joseph. "La Poésie du Jules de Rességuier." *Les Annales Romantiques: Revue d'Histoire du Romantisme* 10, 81–100, 205–27, 341–59.

Defoe, Daniel. *The History of the Wars, of his Present Majesty Charles XII. King of Sweden; From his First Landing in Denmark, to his Return from Turkey to Pomerania by a Scots Gentleman in the Swedish service.* London, 1715.

Delacroix, Eugène. *Journal de Eugene Delacroix.* Ed. by André Joubin. Paris, 1932.

de Rességuier, Jules, le Cte. *Tableaux poétiques.* 4th ed. Paris, 1829.

Dontsov, D. *Pokhid Karla XII na Ukrainy.* London: The Union of Ukrainians in Great Britain, 1955.

Doroshenko, Dmytro. *Bie Ukraine und das Reich, neun jahrhunderte deutsch-ukrainisches beziehungen im spiegel der deutschen wissenschaft und literatur.* Leipzig, 1941.

——. *A Survey of Ukrainian Historiography.* The Ukrainian Academy of Arts and Sciences in the U.S., Inc., 5–6 (1957): 1–435.

Dorville, André Constant. *Memoires d'Azéma, contenant diverses anecdotes des Règnes de Pierre le Grand, Empéreur de Russie, et de l'Impératrice Catherine son Epouse, traduit du russe.* Amsterdam, 1764.

Drahomanov, Mykhalo. *Politichni Pisni Ukrainskogo Narodu.* Geneva, 1883.

Dubitsky, I. V. "Mazepa v zakhodnoevropeiskikh literaturakh." *Trizub* 40–41 (October 17, 1937): 15–18.

Eistricher, Karl. *Polnische Bibliographie des XV–XVII. Jahrhunderts,* part 2, vol. I. Cracow, 1883.

Engel, Johann Christian. *Geschichte der Ukraine und des Cosaken.* Halle, 1796.

Englaender, D. *Lord Byrons Mazeppa: eine Studie.* Berlin, 1897.

Escarpit, Robert. *Lord Byron: un tempérament littéraire.* Paris, 1955.

Escholier, Raymond. *Delacroix: peintre, graveur, écrivain.* Paris, 1926.

Estève, V. E. *Byron et le romantisme français.* Paris, 1907.

[Etty, Robert.] *The Cossack: a Poem, in Three Cantos.* London, 1815.

Evstafiev, Aleksei Grigorevich. *Reflections, Notes, and Original Anecdotes; illustrating the Character of Peter the Great to which is added, a Tragedy in Five Acts, entitled, Alexis, the Czarevitz.* Boston, 1814.

Fiszman, Samuel. *Droga Mickiewicza i Puszkina do historyzmu romantycznego.* Warsaw, 1964.

Foy de la Neuville. *Relation curieuse et nouvelle de Moscovie, contenant l'état présent de cet empire, les expéditions des Moscovites en Crimée, en 1689, les causes des dernières révolutions, leurs moeurs et leurs religion, le récit d'un voyage de Spatarus, par terre à la Chine.* Paris, 1698.

Galster, Bohdan. "Powieść poetycka Rylejewa." *Slavia Orientalis* 10 (1961): 3–30.

Géricault raconté par lui-même et par ses amis. Ed. by Pierre Caillou. Vesenaz-Genève, 1947.

Géricault dans les collections privées françaises: Exposition organisée à bénéfice de la Société des Amis du Louvre, 6 novembre–7 décembre 1964 by Claude Aubry.

Gleckner, Robert F. *Byron and the Ruins of Paradise.* Baltimore: Johns Hopkins Press, 1967.

Grant, Elliott M. *Victor Hugo: a Select and Critical Bibliography.* Chapel Hill: University of North Carolina Press, 1967.

Hill, Aaron. *The Works of the Late Aaron Hill, Esq.; in four volumes.* London, 1753.

Hofmann, Werner. *Das irdische Paradies.* Munich: Prestel, 1960.

———. *The Earthly Paradise: Art in the Nineteenth Century.* Tr. by Brian Battershaw. New York: G. Braziller, 1961.

Holubnycky, Lydia. "Mazepa in Byron's Poem and in History." *The Ukrainian Quarterly* 15 (1959): 336–45.

Hough, Graham. *Image and Experience.* Lincoln: University of Nebraska Press, 1960.

Hrusjevskyj, H. "Do portreta Mazepy." *ZNTS,* 92 (1909): 246–48.

Hugo, Victor. *Les Orientales.* Ed. by Elisabeth Barineau. Paris, 1952–54.

———. *Oeuvres complètes de Victor Hugo.* Ed. by Ollendorff. 45 vols. Paris, 1904–13.

Huyghe, René. *Delacroix.* New York: H. N. Abrams, 1963.

Jarecki, Kazimierz. *Do genezy "Mazepy."* Warsaw, 1903.

Jensen, Alfred. *Mazepa: Historiska Bilder Från Ukraina och Karl XII:s Dagar.* Lund, 1909.

———. "Mazepa in der modernen europaischen Dichtung." *Ukrainische Rundschau,* no. 7 (1909): 299–305.

Journal de Genève, No. 59 (1833), portrait no. 68.

Juliusz Słowacki 1809–1849, księga zbiorowa w stulecie zgonu. London: The Polish Research Center Ltd., 1951.

Juliusz Słowacki w stopiecdziesięciolecie urodziń: materiały i szkice. Warsaw, 1959.

Kentrschynskyi, Bohdan. *Mazepa.* Stockholm, 1962.

Kievskaja Starina 6 (July 1883): 592–96.

Kleiner, Juliusz. "Anegdota o przygodzie milosnej Byrona jednym z zródel Mazepy." *Pamiętnik Literacki* 35(1938): 200.

———. *Juliusz Słowacki, dzieje twórczości.* Paris, 1927.

Koebling, E. "D. Englaender, Lord Byrons Mazeppa." *Englische Studien* 24 (1898): 448–58.

Korschay, Paul. *Englische Literatureinflusse bei Puschkin.* Innsbruck, 1958.

Krupnyckyj, Borys. *Geschichte der Ukraine von den anfangen bis zum jahre 1917.* Wiesbaden, 1963.

———. *Hetman Mazepa und seine Zeit (1687–1709).* Leipzig, 1942.

———. "The Mazeppists." *The Ukrainian Quarterly* 4 (1948): 204–14.

———. "Mazeppa and Soviet Historiographers." *Ukrainsky Zbirnik* 2 (1959): 49–53.

Lednicki, Wacław. *Pouchkine et la Pologne: à propos de la trilogie antipolonaise de Pouchkine.* Paris, 1928.

Lednicki, Wacław. *Pushkin's "Bronze Horseman": the Story of a Masterpiece with an Appendix including, in English, Mickiewcz's "Digression," Pushkin's "Bronze Horseman," and other poems.* Berkeley: University of California Press, 1955.

Lenobl', G. M. *Istoriia i literature.* Moscow, 1960.

Lepnicki, E. "Byron im befreiungskampfe der polnischen National-literatur." *Magazin fur die Literatur des Auslandes,* no. 20 (May 19, 1877): 301–4; no. 21 (May 26, 1877): 317–20; no. 22 (June 2, 1877): 334–36.

Lew, Wasyl. "Mazepa in Slavic Literature." *Slavic and East European Studies* 5 (1960): 200–8.

Lewickyj, W. "Mazeppa in der deutschen Literatur." *Ruthenische Revue* 2 (1904): 596–600, 611–15, 637–44.

Lipiński, Wacław, ed., *Z Dziejow ukrainy ku czci Włodzimierza Antonowicza, Paulina Swiecekiego, i Tadeusza Rylskiego.* Kiev, 1912.

Luciw, Wasyl. *Hetman Ivan Mazepa (zhittia i podvigi Velikogo Hetmana) z mapami i iliustratsiami v teksti.* Toronto, 1954.

Lużny, Ryszard. "Stefan Jaworski—poeta nieznany." *Slavia Orientalis* 16 (1967): 363–76.

Mackiw, Theodore. "A Biographical Sketch of Prince Mazeppa (1639–1709)." *Ukrainian Review* 12 (Winter 1965): 60–83.

——. "Mazeppa (1632–1709) in Contemporary German Sources." *ZNTS* (New York, 1959), paper no. 9.

——. "Mazepa in the Light of Contemporary English and American Sources." *The Ukrainian Quarterly* 15 (1959): 346–62.

——. "Mazepa or Mazeppa?" *Ukrainian Review* 10 (Winter 1963): 42–46.

Magarshack, David. *Pushkin: a Biography.* London: Chapman & Hall, 1967.

Maginn, William. "John Gilpin and Mazeppa." *Blackwoods Magazine* 5 (1819): 434–39.

Maksymovich, Mikhaylo. *Sobranie Sochinenii.* Kiev, 1876.

Malaniuk, E. *Illustrissimus Dominus Mazepa—tlo i postat.* New York: Visnyka, 1960.

Manning, Clarence A. *Hetman of Ukraine: Ivan Mazeppa.* New York: Bookman Associates, 1957.

——. "Mazepa in English Literature." *The Ukrainian Quarterly* 15 (1959): 133–44.

——. *The Story of the Ukraine.* New York: Philosophical Library, 1947.

Marchand, Leslie A. *Byron: a Biography.* 3 vols. New York: Knopf, 1957.

——. *Byron's Poetry: a Critical Introduction.* Boston: Houghton Mifflin, 1965.

Marshall, William H. "A Reading of Byron's *Mazeppa.*" *MLN,* 76 (February 1961): 120–24.

——. *The Structure of Byron's Major Poems.* Philadelphia: University of Pennsylvania Press, 1962.

Martineau, René. "Ernest Fouinet et 'Les Orientales.' " *Mercure de France* (June 16, 1919): 648–59.

Mazeppa: Zbirnik 46–47 (1938–39). Published by Prace Ukrainskiego Instytuto Naukowego in Warsaw.

Mazeppa, Ivan. *Pisannya.* Cracow, 1943.

Mazeppa Travestied: a Poem, with an introductory Address to the goddess of "Milling," and her worshipper, "The Fancy." London, 1820.

"Mazepa v chuzhii literaturi." *Kalendar Svobody* (1959): 77–78.

Milner, Henry M. *Mazeppa; or, the Wild Horse of Tartary.* London, n.d.

Mirsky, D. S. *Pushkin.* New York: Dutton, 1963.

Moore, John Robert. *A Checklist of the Writings of Daniel Defoe.* Bloomington: Indiana University Press, 1960.

Murray, John. *Lord Byron's Correspondence.* New York: C. Scribner's Sons, 1922.

Muśnicki, Nicodemus, S. J. *Pułtawa; poemat epiczny*. Warsaw, 1803.

Niemcewicz, Julian Ursyn. *Spiewy historyczne z muzyką i rycinami*. Warsaw, 1816.

Nodier, Charles. *Annales* 12 (1823): 196–97.

Ohloblyn, Oleksander. *Hetman Ivan Mazepa ta jaho doba*. New York: Organization for the Defense of the Four Ukrainian Freedoms, 1960.

——. "Western Europe and the Ukrainian Baroque: an Aspect of the Cultural Influence at the Time of Hetman Mazepa." *The Annals of the Ukrainian Academy of Arts and Sciences in the U.S.* 1 (1951): 127–37.

Orlik, Philippe. *Déduction des droits de l'Ukraine d'après un ms. conservé dans les archives du château de Dinteville, publié par E. Bortshak*. Lvov, 1925.

Overmyer, Grace. *America's First Hamlet*. New York: New York University Press, 1957.

Partridge, Eric. *The French Romantics' Knowledge of English Literature 1820–48*. Paris, 1924.

Pasek, Jan Chrzystom. *Pamiętniki*. Ed. by Bronislaw Gubrynowicz. Lvov, 1898.

Pauls, John. "Two Treatments of Mazeppa: Ryleyev's and Pushkin's." *Slavic and East European Studies* 7 (1963): 97–109.

——. *Pushkin's Dedication of "Poltava" and Princess Marija Volkonskaya*. Marquette Univ. Slavic Institute Paper no. 12, 1961.

——. *Pushkin's "Poltava."* New York: Shevchenko Scientific Society, 1962.

——. "The Tragedy of Motrya Kochubey." *Ukrainian Review* 12 (Autumn 1965): 78–83.

Payne, John Howard. *Trial without Jury and Other Plays*. Ed. by Cadman Hislop and W. R. Richardson. Princeton: Princeton University Press, 1940.

Peckham, Morse, ed. *Romanticism: the Culture of the Nineteenth Century*. New York: G. Braziller, 1965.

Prokopovich, Feofan. *Sochinenia*. Ed. by I. P. Eremina. Moscow-Leningrad, 1961.

Pushkin, Alexander S. *Pushkin o literature*. ed. by N. V. Bogoslavsky. Moscow-Leningrad, 1934.

——. *The Letters of Alexander Pushkin*. Ed. and tr. by J. Thomas Shaw. Bloomington: Indiana University Press, 1963.

——. *Pushkin polnoe sobranie sochinenii*. Moscow, 1949.

——. *Poltava; poema Aleksandra Pushkina*. St. Petersburg, 1829.

——. *Sobranie sochinenii*. Moscow, 1960.

Quennell, Peter. *Byron: a Self Portrait*. London: J. Murray, 1950.

Raszewski, Zbigniew. *Prace o literaturze i teatrze ofiarowane Zygmuntowi Szweykowskiemu*. Warsaw, 1966.

——. "Słowacki i Mickiewicz wobec teatru romantycznego." *Pamiętnik Teatralny* 1–3 (1959): 12.

——. *Staroswięćczyzna i postęp czasu*. Warsaw, 1963.

Rich, Vera. "Two Poems of Hetman Ivan Mazeppa." *Ukrainian Review* 6 (Autumn 1959): 46–8.

Riffaterre, Michael. "Hugo's *Orientales* Revisited." *American Society Legion of Honor Magazine* 36, no. 2, pp. 103–18.

Robaut, Alfred. *L'Oeuvre complète de Eugène Delacroix*. Paris, 1885.

Romantyzm: studia nad sztuka drugiej poł., w. XVIII i w. XIX, materiały sesji Stow. Historyków Sztuki. Warsaw, 1967.

Rosenthal, Léon. *L'Art et les artistes romantiques*. Paris, 1928.

——. *La Peinture romantique: essai sur l'évaluation de la peinture française de 1815 à 1830*. Paris, n.d.

Rudowska, Stanslawa. *L'Enfance et la jeunesse de Bohdan Zaleski*. Vienna, 1915.

Ryleev, Kondratii Federovich. *Voynarovsky sochinenie K. Ryleeva.* Moskva, 1825.
———. *Stikhotvorenia, stati, ocherki, dokladnie zapiski, pisma.* Moscow, 1956.
———. *Wojnarowski.* Tr. by Władysława Sykrokomli and Włodzimierz Slobodnik, with
    intro. by Leon Gomolicki. Wrocław, 1955.
Seché, Léon. *Le Cénacle de Joseph Delorme (1827–30): Victor Hugo et les poètes de "Cromwell" a
    "Hernani"; Victor Hugo et les artistes.* Paris, 1912.
Seven Britons in Imperial Russia 1698–1812. Ed. by Peter Putnam. Princeton: Princeton Uni-
    versity Press, 1952.
Shutoy, V. "The Treason of Mazepa." *Istoricheskii Zapiski,* no. 31 (1950): 154–90.
Simmons, Ernest J. "La littérature anglaise et Pouchkine." *Revue de Littérature Comparée* 17
    (January 1937): 79–107.
———. *Pushkin.* Cambridge, Mass.: Harvard University Press, 1937.
Sitjynsky, Volodimir. "Avtentytjnyj portret Hetman Mazepy." *Ukrajina* 3 (Paris, 1950):
    192–94.
Słowacki, Juliusz. *Dzieje Wszystkie.* Ed. by Juliusz Kleiner. Wrocław, 1958.
———. *Kalendarz zycia i twórcości.* Ed. by E. Sawrymowicz. Wrocław, 1962–63.
———. *Mazepa.* Ed. by Bronisław Gubrynowicz. Cracow, 1924.
———. *Mazepa.* Ed. by Kazimierz Zimmermann. Lvov, 1895.
———. *Sądy współczesnych o twórcości Słowackiego.* Ed. by Bogdan Zakrzewski, Kazimierz
    Pecold i Artur Ciemnoczołowski. Wrocław, 1963.
Tatar, Marian. "Stan badań na twórczoscią Juliusza Słowackiego w latach 1945–1960."
    Pamiętnik Literacki 55 (1964): 261–310, 505–59.
Tezla, Albert. "Byron's Oriental Tales: a Critical Study." Dissertation, University of
    Chicago, 1953.
Thorslev, Peter. *The Byronic Hero: Types and Prototypes.* Minneapolis: University of Min-
    nesota Press, 1962.
Treugutt, Stefan. *Juliusz Słowacki: Romantic Poet.* Warsaw, 1959.
———. *Pisarska młodość Słowackiego.* Wrocław, 1958.
Troyat, Henri. *Pouchkine: Biographie.* Paris, 1953.
Tseytlin, A. G. *Tvorchestva Ryleyeva.* Moscow, 1955.
Ujejski, Jozef. *Antoni Malczewski: poeta i poemat.* Warsaw, 1921.
Ukraine: a Concise Encyclopedia. Toronto: University of Toronto Press, 1963.
Varnecke, B. V. *History of the Russian Theater: Seventeenth through Nineteenth Century.* New
    York: Macmillan, 1951.
Vickery, Walter N. "Parallelizm v literaturnom razvitii Bajrona i Pushkina." *American Con-
    tributions to the Fifth International Congress of Slavists, Sofia, September, 1963.*
———. "Three Examples of Narrated Speech in Pushkin's Poltava." *The American Slavic
    and East European Journal* 7 (n.s.): 278–83.
Victor Hugo raconté par un témoin de sa vie. Paris, 1864.
Vogué, Eugène Melchior. *Trois drames de l'histoire de Russie: le fils de Pierre le Grand.* Paris,
    1911.
Voltaire, François Marie Arouet. *Oeuvres complètes de Voltaire.* 52 vols. Paris, 1877–85.
———. *The Works of Voltaire, a Contemporary Version, with notes by Tobias Smollett, revised and
    modernized new translations by William F. Fleming, and an introduction by Oliver H. G.
    Leigh.* New York: St. Hubert Guild, 1901.
White, Orville. "Lord Byron's Use and Conception of History." Dissertation, University
    of North Carolina, 1954.
Zaleski, Bohdan. *Piesni polskie i ruskie ludu galicyjskiego.* Lvov, 1833.

Zaslavsky, I. *Ryleev i rosiiski-ukrainski literaturni vzaemni.* Kiev, 1958.
Zhirmunskii, Viktor M. *Bajron i Pushkin.* Leningrad, 1924.
———. "Stikh i perevod: iz istoria romanticheskoi poemy." *American Contributions to the Fifth International Congress of Slavists, Sofia, September, 1963.*

INDEX